VISIONS IN CONFLICT
Peacebuilding in Cyprus: A View from the Ground

A. Marco Turk

(Prologue by Joseph S. Joseph)

Visions in Conflict Volume II

Portions of this book have appeared in Loyola of Los Angeles International & Comparative Law Review. Copyright (c) 2006, 2007, and 2009 by Loyola of Los Angeles International & Comparative Law Review. Reprinted with permission of publisher.

Copyright 2013 by Brian C. Alston, Publisher
Requests for Information should be addressed to:
Brian C. Alston, P.O. Box 3170 Lihue, HI 96766

(Under Library of Congress)
Turk, A. Marco (Avrum Marco), 1935-
Visions in conflict - Peacebuilding in Cyprus: A view from the ground
ISBN-10: 1439268584

Series Editor Brian C. Alston
Cover Artist John Barbour
Author's Photo by Stacie Isabella Turk
Printed in the United States of America

2

TABLE OF CONTENTS

ACKNOWLEDGEMENTS

I owe an enormous debt to all of the people of Cyprus on both sides of the island with whom I have worked since 1997, especially those who risked personal retaliation for their participation in the bi-communal activities that I conducted over the years and who have since become my friends, still maintaining regular contact. My wife, Kathryn, shares in this venture because she gave up her career to join me in Cyprus at the start of this odyssey, and in the years since she has been bedrock of support while I have continued that work.

My appreciation goes out to Brian Alston for his support and suggestion that this book be published as Volume II in the *Visions of Conflict* series, and to Kirstin Ericson, 2010-2011 Editor-in-Chief of the *Loyola of Los Angeles International & Comparative Law Review,* where my three law review articles on the Cyprus Problem have been published (Vol. 28, No. 2, 205-255 [2006]; Vol. 29, No. 3, 463-501 [2007]; Vol. 31, No. 3, 327-362 [2009]), for her gracious permission to collect those articles as the basis for this book. I am grateful to Shawn Tafreshi, who, as then Editor-in-Chief of the law review and formerly my UC Irvine undergraduate student, enthusiastically solicited the first of the three articles that started this journey and who provided the structural suggestions that I utilized therein. The smooth start to, and continued motivation for, attainment of academic excellence in my career as a full-time educator must be attributed to Dr. Henry Pontell (my first department chair) and Dr. John Dombrink (my first mentor) from the Department of Criminology, Law and Society, School of Social Ecology, at UC Irvine. A portion of the material in this book, before appearing in the first of my three law review articles, appeared in my lead article, *Democratized Restorative Justice as a Lesson for*

Criminology: Cyprus 1997-2003, published in *The Criminologist,* Vol. 29 (3), 1, 3-4 [May/June 2004]. I wish to express my appreciation to the then editor (Dr. Pontell) of *The Criminologist* for permission to re-use that material.

Without the opportunity provided by the Cyprus Fulbright Commission and the full support of its Executive Director, Daniel Hadjittofi, and his staff, I would not have been able to achieve the success that I did working with the bi-communal participants on the island. While in that pursuit, I was fortunate to make the acquaintance and secure the friendship of Dr. Joseph S. Joseph who is Jean Monnet Professor of International Relations and European Affairs at the University of Cyprus, currently serving as Cyprus Ambassador to Greece. I am deeply indebted to him for his willingness to provide the prologue to this book after becoming acquainted with my series of Loyola Law School/Los Angeles law review articles.

Finally, I acknowledge with affection the memory of my parents, Harry and Helen, who set the bar for my efforts to make a difference in the lives of others, and my daughters, Hillary and Stacie, who have been enthusiastic cheerleaders.

A. Marco Turk
Santa Monica, California
July 2013

ABOUT THE AUTHOR

A. Marco Turk is Emeritus Professor of Negotiation, Conflict Resolution and Peacebuilding, and the director (2002-2010, 2012-2013) who specifically designed that program at California State University Dominguez Hills. The honor of emeritus status was awarded in 2010 in recognition of the abundant contributions he has made to the students and to the institution during his many years as a member of the faculty at that university. He has also served as an adjunct professor of law at Loyola Law School/Los Angeles, teaching international conflict resolution, both domestically (2007) and in Cyprus (2012). His degrees are BA (Bachelor of Arts) in Political Science from the University of Washington (Seattle), and his JD (Doctor of Law) *cum laude* is from Southwestern University School of Law (Los Angeles).

Professor Turk's areas of emphasis are mediator ethics, and restorative justice and peacebuilding in ethnically divided communities. With a long history in California alternative dispute resolution and recognized internationally for his work as a peacebuilder, educator and trainer dealing with ethnic conflict, he was a Fulbright Senior Scholar in Conflict Resolution on Cyprus (1997-1999), has made funded return trips in 2000, 2001, 2003, 2005, and 2008 to continue his peacebuilding work there, and he has conducted programs for Cypriots in the USA through the US State Department and the Fred J. Hansen Institute for World Peace at San Diego State University. In October 2003, Professor Turk was one of two

Americans invited to attend the Oxford University international workshop on "Getting to Yes," regarding efforts to reunify Cyprus. In 2011, he was nominated by the provost and vice president for academic affairs, upon recommendation of the deans, as the California State University Dominguez Hills candidate for the 2011-2012 Brandeis University Gittler Prize, as a "quintessential faculty member from this University, who has dedicated the last 14 years to the study and production of a body of published work that reflects scholarly excellence and a lasting contribution to the understanding and hopeful resolution of ethnic conflict on the Island of Cyprus."

Prologue by Joseph S. Joseph[1]

The Cyprus Problem: An Overview

Introduction

The purpose of this prologue is to provide an overview and essential background of the Cyprus problem which can serve as a basis for the chapters which follow. In doing so, it provides a basic context and an analysis of the political developments that followed the declaration of independence in 1960. Emphasis is placed on the historical, geographical, social, cultural, institutional, and political roots of the conflict on the island. The role of Greece and Turkey (the motherlands) is also examined. It also looks briefly at the efforts and prospects for a settlement, especially now that Cyprus is a member of the European Union.

In recent decades, the Cyprus problem has gone through three phases. Until 1960, it was a colonial issue which was settled with the declaration of independence and the establishment of the Republic of Cyprus. From 1960 to

---

[1] *Joseph S. Joseph* is Jean Monnet Professor of International Relations and European Affairs at the University of Cyprus, and served as Ambassador of Cyprus to Greece from September 2009 to August 2013. He received his BA from Panteion University (Greece), MA from the University of Stockholm (Sweden), and PhD from Miami University (USA). He was a postdoctoral fellow at Harvard and taught at the University of Alabama, Gustavus Adolphus College (Minnesota) and Miami University. He has published extensively (books, chapters and articles in scholarly books and international journals) on international relations, the European Union, Cyprus and EU-Turkish relations.

1974, the problem was essentially an internal dispute between the Greek Cypriots and the Turkish Cypriots in which external powers became involved – primarily Greece, Turkey, and Britain, the guarantor powers of the independence of Cyprus under the 1960 settlement, but also, during the second phase, the United States and the Soviet Union, by virtue of their superpower status. The third phase covers the period from 1974 to the present: following the Greek coup and the Turkish invasion of Cyprus in 1974, the dominant element of the problem has been the de facto division of the island and the continuing occupation of its northern part by Turkey.

Geographical and Historical Setting

Three geographical characteristics of Cyprus have determined much of its fate: location, size and the fact that it is an island. It is the island in the eastern Mediterranean, located at a strategic position at the crossroads of three continents. Its strategic location, long exposed coastline, and small size (3,572 square miles, 9,851 square kilometers) always made it an attractive and easy target for outsiders. Its historical and demographic records reflect the ebb and flow of peoples and powers in the region. As Alan James aptly points out, "[t]hroughout recorded time, its political experience has reflected the interlocking impact of two utterly basic geographic factors: size and location. From their influence the island has been wholly unable to escape."[2] In the course of its long history, Cyprus has been conquered by most of the major powers that had interest in, or sought control of, the Middle East. The list of its successive rulers include the Egyptians, Greeks, Phoenicians, Assyrians, Persians, Ptolemies, Romans,

---

[2] Alan James, *Keeping the Peace in the Cyprus Crisis of 1963-64* (London: Palgrave, 2002), p. 3.

Byzantines, Franks, Venetians, Ottoman Turks, and British. It gained its independence from Britain in 1960.

Among these rulers, only the Greeks and the Turks had a significant lasting demographic impact on Cypriot society. The Greeks settled on the island during the second half of the second millennium BC. The Turks settled in Cyprus following the Ottoman occupation of the island in 1571. Under the Cyprus convention which was signed at the Congress of Berlin in 1878, the sultan ceded Cyprus to Britain, which was to administer the island in exchange for a promise to help Turkey defend itself against Russian expansion. In 1914, at the onset of the Second World War and after Turkey had joined forces with the Central Powers, Britain declared the 1878 convention null and annexed Cyprus. With the 1923 peace treaty of Lausanne, Turkey officially recognized the annexation of Cyprus by Britain and the island was proclaimed a colony of the British crown in 1925.

By 1878, when the British took control of the island, the bi-communal character of Cypriot society had been formed and consolidated. During the 82 years of British rule no major demographic change took place on the island. In 1960, its population was approximately 570,000, consisting of roughly 80 percent Greeks and 20 percent Turks.[3] There were purely Greek, purely Turkish, and mixed settlements in all regions of the island. There were (and still are) also small ethnic groups of Armenians, Maronites, and Latins living in Cyprus.[4]

---

[3] According to the 1960 census, the population of Cyprus was 572,707, distributed as follows: Greek Cypriots 447,901 (78.20%); Turkish Cypriots 103,822 (18.13%); Other (mainly Maronites, Armenians and Latins) 20,984 (3.66%).

[4] For detailed statistics and an extensive analysis of the demography of Cyprus at the time of independence, see L.W. St. John Jones, *The Population of Cyprus* (London: Maurice Temple Smith, 1983).

Roots of Sociopolitical Differentiation

The Greek Cypriots and the Turkish Cypriots have been divided along linguistic, ethnic, cultural, and religious lines. The Greek Cypriots speak Greek and identify with the Greek nation, Greek culture, and the heritage of classical Greece and the Byzantine Empire. Almost all of them are members of the Orthodox Church of Cyprus, which is an autocephalous member of the Greek Eastern Orthodox Church. The Turkish Cypriots speak Turkish and identify with the Turkish nation, Turkish culture, and the heritage of the Turkish Ottoman Empire. Virtually all of them are Moslems of the Sunni sect.[5]

Despite four centuries of coexistence and considerable physical intermingling, the two communities remained separate and distinct ethnic groups. It should be recalled that the current spatial distribution of the two groups was to come later: a partial physical separation of the two communities took place with the eruption of intercommunal violence in 1963, and an almost complete separation came into effect after the Turkish invasion of Cyprus in 1974, with the result that by 2010 there are only a few hundred Greek Cypriots living in the Turkish occupied part and about a thousand Turkish Cypriots in the south. During the period of Ottoman and British rule, certain factors contributed to the preservation of the linguistic, ethnic, cultural, and religious characteristics of the two communities and the creation of a political cleavage along ethnic lines.

The Orthodox Church, which maintained a dominant position among the Greek Cypriots, helped them

---

[5] For a variety of perspectives and insightful analyses on the history, culture and demography of Cyprus, see the collective volume Vangelis Calotychos, ed., *Cyprus and Its People: Nation, and Experience in an Unimaginable Community, 1955-1997* (Boulder, CO: Westview Press, 1998).

preserve their religious, ethnic, cultural, and political identity. When the Ottomans conquered Cyprus from the Venetians in 1571, they destroyed the Roman Catholic Church and elevated the Greek Orthodox Church to a position of supremacy in the island. The autonomy of the Orthodox Church was confirmed and the archbishop was recognized as the religious and political leader of the Greek Cypriot community.[6] For the Greek Cypriots, the church became a symbol of political and ethnic unity. Most of their political, social, cultural, and intellectual life was associated with religious activities and institutions. The church continued to be the most prominent institution of the Greek Cypriots under British rule.

The Ottoman *millet* administrative system distinguished the two communities on the basis of religion and ethnicity.[7] According to this system, which was applied throughout the Ottoman Empire, each religious ethnic group was treated as a distinct entity. Taxes were imposed on a denominational basis and administration was carried out with the help of the various religious institutions. The Ottoman conquerors restored the Orthodox Church of Cyprus with this aim in mind. The administrative separation of the Greek Cypriots and the Turkish Cypriots helped them maintain their ethnic identity, but it also contributed to the politicization of ethnicity. When the British took control of Cyprus, the *millet* system was not

---

[6] In the seventeenth century the sultan of the Ottoman Empire granted the title of ethnarch (ethnic political leader) to the archbishop of Cyprus. Thus, the religious leader became also *ex officio* political leader of the Greek Cypriot community. That practice remained unchanged until Cyprus became independent in 1960. That explains, to some degree, why it was easy for Archbishop Makarios to win the first presidential elections and become the first president of Cyprus.

[7] The word *millet* is of Arabic origin. It appears in the Koran with the meaning of religion. In the Ottoman Empire it came to mean ethnic/religious group.

completely abolished. A modern bureaucratic administration was established, but the two ethnic groups retained control in matters of religion, education, culture, personal status, and communal institutions.

The divisive educational system perpetuated ethnic distinctiveness by transferring conflicting ethnic values from generation to generation. The two communities had separate schools which were, to some degree, controlled by their respective religious institutions. Throughout the Ottoman period and the early years of British rule, Orthodox and Moslem priests were also school teachers. During the period of British rule, the curricula of the Cypriot schools were similar to those in Greece or Turkey. They placed emphasis on religion, national heritage (of Greece and Turkey respectively – not of Cyprus), ethnic values, and the long history of Greek-Turkish rivalry.

The two Cypriot communities had antagonistic loyalties to Greece and Turkey. Each community honored the national holidays, played the national anthem, and used the flag of its mother country. Cypriots from both ethnic groups fought as volunteers on opposite sides during the 1912-13 Balkan wars, the First World War, and the Greek-Turkish war of 1919-23. Attachment to two rival and often belligerent countries promoted ethnic distinctiveness and served as an instrument for the transplantation of the wider Greek-Turkish confrontation into Cyprus.

The two ethnic groups held conflicting views about the political future of the island. Throughout the British period, *enosis* (union of Cyprus with Greece) was the most persistent and rigid goal of the Greek Cypriots.[8] It could be

---

[8] The idea of *enosis* dates back to the creation of the Modern Greek state in 1830. It became a political issue when the British took control of Cyprus in 1878. Under Ottoman rule its propagation was not allowed. The Greek Cypriots saw the change from Ottoman to British rule as a first step toward the achievement of *enosis*. For accounts on

15

seen as part of the wider Panhellenic movement of *megali idea* (great idea) which aimed at reconstruction of the Byzantine Empire. On the Turkish side, the idea of *taksim* (partition of Cyprus into Greek and Turkish sections) was advanced as a counter force to *enosis*. Both movements were supported by Greece and Turkey respectively. Attachment to the conflicting goals of *enosis* and *taksim* led to a political polarization between the two ethnic groups.

The British colonial policy of "divide and rule" maintained and reinforced the ethnic, administrative, and political separation inherited from the Ottoman period. The British administration made no effort to create a unifying Cypriot political culture. The two communities were treated as separate groups for administrative purposes and antagonism between them was stirred.[9] The maintenance of a psychological and administrative gap between the two ethnic groups was instrumental in securing British control over Cyprus.

The above factors – church dominance, *millet* system, fragmented ethnic education, antagonistic national loyalties, political polarization, and the British policy of "divide and rule" – contributed to the preservation of the ethnic identity of the two Cypriot communities and the generation of a political schism between them. Four

the emergence of the idea of *enosis* and the evolution of the *enosis* movement see Anita Walker, "Enosis in Cyprus: Dhali, a Case Study," *Middle East Journal* Vol. 38, No. 3 (Summer 1984): 474-94; and Michael Attalides, *Cyprus: Nationalism and International Politics* (New York: St. Martin's Press, 1979), pp. 22-35.

[9] Two measures illustrating the segregationist character of the British policy may be given as examples. First, the Greek and Turkish members of the legislative council were elected separately by the two communities. Second, during the Greek Cypriot revolt against British colonial rule (1955-1959), a special police consisting primarily of Turkish Cypriots was set up by the colonial administration to fight the Greek Cypriot guerillas.

centuries of geographic proximity and physical intermingling did not produce intercommunal bonds strong enough to counteract the divisive effects of religious, administrative, educational, social, and cultural distinctiveness. Communal segregation was further reinforced by mutual suspicion, fear, and uncertainty "for which one might coin the term 'postjudices,' since they are based upon close observation and not ignorant misconception."[10] It was on these fragmented historical and social foundations that an independent bi-communal Cypriot state was built in 1960.

Establishment of the Republic of Cyprus

Britain granted independence to Cyprus in 1960, giving way to pressure from three different directions. First, there was a bloody Greek Cypriot anti-colonial revolt, which lasted from 1955 to 1959, causing much trouble for the British authorities and making the administration of the island a difficult and costly task. The revolt, which took the form of a guerilla war, was spearheaded by the Orthodox Church under the leadership of Archbishop Makarios and the underground National Organization of Cypriot Fighters (*Ethnike Organosis Kyprion Agoniston*, EOKA) under the leadership of its founder General George Grivas Dighenis. The revolt was carried out in the name of *enosis* and had the support of Greece. Turkey and the Turkish Cypriots, on the other hand, were demanding partition. Some incidents of ethnic violence occurred and further tension was generated between Greece and Turkey.[11]

---

[10] H. D. Purcell, *Cyprus* (New York: Praeger, 1968), p. 245.

[11] For detailed accounts on domestic and international developments during the period 1955-59, see Robert Holland, *Britain and the Revolt in Cyprus* (Oxford: Clarendon Press, 1998); and Nancy Crawshaw, *The Cyprus Revolt: An Account of the Struggle for Union with Greece* (London: Allen and Unwin, 1978).

17

Second, there was global pressure resulting from the internationalization of the Cyprus issue, especially at the UN, in the context of the broader anti-colonial movement and decolonization process that were sweeping the world in the 1950s. The issue was taken to the UN General Assembly in five consecutive years, from 1954 to 1958.[12] Appeals to the UN were made by Greece, asking for application of the principles of equal rights and self-determination in Cyprus. The Greek appeals were supported by the Eastern (Soviet) bloc and the third world countries. Greece also asked for *enosis* "in view of the repeatedly and solemnly expressed will of the overwhelming majority of the people of Cyprus for union with Greece, which they regard as their mother country."[13] The General Assembly made a recommendation for a peaceful solution of the Cyprus colonial problem in accordance with the principles of the UN Charter.

Third, American pressure was applied to Britain, Greece, and Turkey to seek a solution to the Cyprus problem and heal the Greek–Turkish "festering sore" within NATO. The US was concerned with the mounting Greek–Turkish tension which threatened to paralyze the southeastern flank of the Western alliance. American concern over Cypriot developments was manifested in unsuccessful initiatives in 1957 and 1958 aiming at a settlement of the problem within NATO.

As a result of the above pressures, a solution to the colonial problem of Cyprus was sought through diplomacy.

---

[12] For a standard work on the Greek appeals to the UN and other developments in the international diplomacy see Stephen Xydis, *Cyprus: Conflict and Reconciliation, 1954-1958* (Columbus: Ohio State University Press, 1967).

[13] UN doc. A/2703, letter dated 16 August 1954, from the Greek prime minister to the secretary-general requesting the inclusion of the Cyprus issue in the agenda of the General Assembly.

Early in 1959, tripartite talks were held in Zurich between Britain, Greece, and Turkey and an agreement was reached for the establishment of an independent Cypriot state, the Republic of Cyprus. Final agreements were signed in London on 19 February 1959, by Britain, Greece, Turkey, and the two Cypriot communities, although the latter did not participate in the negotiations. The problem was, in effect, settled on a bilateral basis between Greece and Turkey under British auspices. Factors and considerations emanating from the ethnic, historical, linguistic, cultural, and religious ties of the two Cypriot ethnic groups with their respective motherlands defined the context and content of the settlement.

The London and Zurich Agreements

The London and Zurich agreements consisted of a series of treaties which laid the foundations of the political structure of the new state. These treaties were the Treaty of Establishment, the Treaty of Alliance, the Treaty of Guarantee, and the agreement on the basic structure of the Republic of Cyprus which contained the key provisions of the constitution which was drafted later. The treaties and the constitution were officially signed on 16 August 1960, in Nicosia and went into effect immediately.[14]

The Treaty of Establishment was aimed at safeguarding British military interests in Cyprus. It provided for two sovereign British military areas of 99 square miles (256 square kilometers).

---

[14] For extensive analyses and interpretations of the legal and political aspects and consequences of the 1960 founding treaties see R. St. J. Macdonald, "International Law and the Conflict on Cyprus", *Canadian Yearbook of International Law* Vol. 29 (1981), pp. 3-49; and Thomas Ehrlich, *Cyprus, 1958-1967: International Crises and the Role of Law* (New York: Oxford University Press, 1974).

The Treaty of Alliance was a defense pact between Greece, Turkey and Cyprus. It provided for the permanent stationing of Greek and Turkish contingents in Cyprus, comprising 950 and 650 men respectively.

With the Treaty of Guarantee Cyprus undertook to "ensure the maintenance of its independence, territorial integrity and security" and prohibit "any activity likely to promote, directly or indirectly, either union with any other State or partition of the Island."[15] Britain, Greece, and Turkey were named guarantor powers of the Republic and were granted the right to take action, jointly or unilaterally, toward "reestablishing the state of affairs created by the present Treaty" in the event of its breach.[16] The Treaty of Guarantee was primarily aimed at mutual abandonment of the conflicting ethno political goals of *enosis* and partition.

The Constitution

The agreement on the basic structure of the Republic of Cyprus contained the key provisions of the constitution which was drafted later and put into effect when the Republic officially came into being. The constitution was based on communal dualism. It provided for the establishment of a bi-communal state and aimed at regulation and protection of the interests of the two communities as distinct ethnic groups. It identified and recognized the two communities by reference to their ethnic origin, language, cultural traditions, and religion.[17] It

---

[15] Treaty of Guarantee, art. 1.

[16] Ibid., art. 4.

[17] Article 2 of the Constitution identified the two communities as follows: "(1) the Greek Community comprises all citizens of the Republic who are of Greek origin and whose mother tongue is Greek or who share the Greek cultural traditions or who are members of the Greek-Orthodox Church; (2) the Turkish Community comprises all citizens of the Republic who are of Turkish origin and whose mother

gave them "the right to celebrate respectively the Greek and Turkish national holidays"[18] and use "the flag of the Republic or the Greek or Turkish flag without any restriction."[19] The two communities were also granted the right to establish separate special relationships with Greece and Turkey on educational, religious, cultural, and athletic matters.

The constitution institutionalized communal dualism in all spheres of government activity. In the executive branch, it provided for a presidential regime, the president being Greek Cypriot and the vice-president Turkish Cypriot, elected separately by the two communities. The council of ministers was composed of seven Greek Cypriots and three Turkish Cypriots. The president appointed the Greek Cypriot and the vice-president the Turkish Cypriot ministers. Decisions by the council of ministers were taken by absolute majority, but the president and the vice-president had the right to veto, jointly or separately, decisions on foreign affairs, defense, and security.

According to the constitution, legislative power was exercised by the House of Representatives and two communal chambers. The House was composed of 35 Greek Cypriots and 15 Turkish Cypriot representatives, elected separately by the two ethnic groups.[20] The president of the House was Greek Cypriot and the vice-president Turkish Cypriot. Laws in the House were passed by simple

---

tongue is Turkish or who share the Turkish cultural traditions or who are Moslems."

[18] Constitution, art. 1.

[19] Ibid., art. 4.

[20] These figures were changed to 56 Greek Cypriots and 24 Turkish Cypriots although, because of the de facto partition of the island, Turkish Cypriots representatives have not been serving in the parliament.

majority, except in the cases of "any modification of the Electoral Law and the adoption of any law relating to the municipalities and of any law imposing duties or taxes", where a separate simple majority of the representatives of the two communities was required.[21] The two communal chambers were independent legislative bodies elected separately by the two communities. They had exclusive legislative power in relation to their respective ethnic groups on the following matters: all religious matters; all educational, cultural, and teaching matters; personal status; administration of justice dealing with civil disputes relating to personal status and religious matters; and in matters where the interests and institutions were purely of a communal nature, such as charitable and sporting institutions. The two chambers could also impose personal taxes and fees on their communities in order to finance communal activities and institutions. Division of the legislative branch meant, in effect, that each ethnic group could run its own affairs independently and in contrast to the interests of the other community.

Communal dualism was also institutionalized in the judicial system. The composition of the lower courts was determined by the communal membership of the disputants. If the plaintiff and the defendant belonged to the same community, the court was composed of judges belonging to that community. The Supreme Court was composed of a Greek Cypriot, a Turkish Cypriot, and a neutral judge. The neutral judge was the president of the court and could not be a citizen of Cyprus, Greece, Turkey, or Britain. The transplantation of ethnic fragmentation into the administration of justice, partly inherited from the colonial period, could undermine the very concept of justice. In an ethnically and politically divided society, ethnic

---

[21] Constitution, art. 78.

considerations could influence the operation of courts and result in undermining of the administration of justice.

The constitution provided for the establishment of separate municipalities: "separate municipalities shall be created in the five largest towns of the Republic.... The Council of the Greek municipality in any such town shall be elected by the Greek electors of the town and the Turkish municipality in such towns shall be elected by the Turkish electors of the town."[22] It is worth mentioning that despite the existence of Greek and Turkish quarters, there was some intermingling of the population in the five towns. Application of this provision could result in movement of populations.

A disproportional communal ratio of participation in the public service, the police, and the armed forces was fixed by the constitution. Although the Greek-Turkish population ratio was roughly 80:20, the public service and the police would be composed of 70 percent Greeks and 30 percent Turks; the ratio in the army was 60:40. The provisions for disproportionate participation of the Turkish Cypriots in the public sector left an opening for a negative reaction among the Greek Cypriots, given its departure from the principle of equal treatment of each and all citizens.

Finally, the constitution provided that provisions incorporated from the Zurich and London accords could not "in any way be amended, whether by way of variation, addition, or repeal."[23] All the constitutional features presented above were among the "basic articles", and so were the treaties of alliance and guarantee that were integral parts of the constitution. In other words, the political framework was not only awkward and unworkable, but also rigid and unalterable. It excluded any

---

[22] Ibid., art. 173.

[23] Ibid., art. 182.

adaptation or evolutionary political process through which the two groups could negotiate, adjust their positions, and seek common ground for reconciliation and a settlement. As a political analyst put it, "it was a constitutional straitjacket precluding that adaptation essential to the growth and survival of any body politic."[24]

It should be noted also that the Republic of Cyprus came into being as a result of international agreements which were reached in the absence of the Cypriot people. The constitution of the new state was imposed on the population; it was never submitted to a referendum. A series of treaties set limitations on the independence, sovereignty, and territorial integrity of the Republic. Foreign powers were granted the right to station military forces on its territory and interfere in its domestic affairs.

The Dysfunctional State

One of the primary tasks of the first government of the Republic was to build the state institutions provided for by the constitution. This, however, proved to be a difficult task. The Greek Cypriots were not enthusiastic about the implementation of some of the constitutional provisions that they regarded as unjust and unrealistic. The Turkish Cypriots, on the other hand, insisted on full implementation of the constitution, especially the provisions regarding their safeguards and privileges. A series of incidents revolving around "basic articles" of the constitution undermined the entire process of state building. After three years of simmering tension and fruitless efforts to establish constitutional order and a working state, a complete constitutional breakdown and eruption of violence occurred in December 1963. The major sources of constitutional

---

[24] Glenn D. Camp, "Greek-Turkish Conflict over Cyprus," *Political Science Quarterly*, Vol. 95, No. 3 (Spring 1980), p. 49.

tension included the provisions for the 70:30 ratio in the public service, the separate majority vote in the parliament, the establishment of separate municipalities, and the right of the president and vice-president to veto decisions of the council of ministers and the parliament.

The 70:30 ratio in the public service was in discordance to the 80:20 ratio of the population. The Greek Cypriots felt that this provision was arbitrary, unjust, and discriminatory, and therefore, it should not be implemented. The Turkish Cypriots, on the other hand, argued that the 70:30 ratio was a restoration of equity in the public service, which had been dominated by the Greek Cypriots under the British administration. Efforts made by President Makarios and Vice-President Kutchuk to find a compromise solution failed and the issue was never settled. From 1960 to 1963, a large number of appointments in the public service were disputed on communal grounds and taken to court. The court, however, could not make any progress toward a settlement of the conflict because it was also paralyzed by ethnic fragmentation and polarization. Its neutral president, German jurist Ernst Forsthoff, found himself caught amidst ethnically polarized factions and resigned in May 1963. Since the conflict was more ethno political than legal in nature, the question of the 70:30 ratio was never resolved. Consequently, the public service could not become fully operational.

The provision for separate majorities in the parliament was another source of ethnic based political tension. The Greek Cypriots felt that the provision violated democratic principles and gave the Turkish Cypriot minority a powerful obstructive weapon. The Turkish Cypriots argued that with the separate majority vote they could protect themselves from Greek Cypriot domination. The confrontation over the separate majority provision led to a communal polarization in the legislative process. As a result, basic laws badly needed for the smooth operation of the state could not pass. This may be illustrated by the case of tax legislation. When the Republic came into being, there was a need for legislation on income tax. The government introduced a bill in parliament to address this, but the Turkish Cypriot representatives used their separate majority right to block it. They justified their position by referring to a delay in the implementation of other constitutional provisions, especially the 70:30 ratio in the public service and the establishment of separate municipalities. Finally, the two communal chambers intervened separately and passed communal laws imposing taxes on their respective ethnic groups. With this development, the two groups moved further apart and the unity of the state and the economy suffered a heavy blow. Taxes were, in effect, imposed on an ethnic basis and used to finance separate communal institutions, projects, and services. The lack of central control or regulation of public financial affairs led to chaos and disarray in the economic life of the new state. Economic paralysis in the public sector had, in turn, a negative impact on the economy and well-being of both communities.

The provision for separate municipalities also caused much trouble, and gave rise to problems which were never resolved. The Greek Cypriots criticized this provision and resisted its implementation. They looked at it with suspicion because it had partitionist connotations and could be seen as a first step toward partition. Needless to say, the handling of the municipal affairs of a city by two competing councils would be inoperable. The issue was brought to the parliament where separate majority votes confirmed the deadlock. Thereafter, the two sides followed different courses of action. The president, backed by the Greek Cypriot dominated council of ministers, issued an executive order calling for the appointment of unified municipal boards. The Turkish Cypriot communal chamber responded by passing a communal law legitimizing separate Turkish municipalities. Both acts were ruled unconstitutional and void *ab initio* by the supreme court. In both instances the vote of the opposite communal judge decided the case. The two sides, however, insisted on their positions, and a settlement on the issue was never reached. The result was chaos and disarray in the municipal affairs of the five largest towns of the island. Diana Markides accurately writes that "[t]he municipal issue, as manifested during this period, was in effect a microcosm of the Cyprus problem. It represented a method of maintaining Turkish political control within the island. Simultaneously, it would give the Turkish Cypriots the element of autonomy they needed to avoid assimilation and discrimination as an impotent minority."[25]

The right granted to the president and vice-president to veto certain decisions of the government and the parliament led to a deadlock in the executive branch. The frequent exercise of the veto right in the government led to disturbing controversies and immobilization of the entire governmental machinery with destructive effects on the functioning of the state and interethnic relations. A major crisis occurred when a decision was made by the council of ministers for the formation of an army on a mixed basis. The vice-president vetoed the decision and asked for the establishment of an army based on separate communal units. He argued that soldiers with linguistic, cultural, religious, and ethnic differences could not be quartered together, and therefore, the army should be ethnically separated. The president reacted by questioning the applicability of the right of veto of the vice-president in that particular case. Then, he went further to declare that under

---

[25] Diana Weston Markides, *Cyprus 1957-1963, From Colonial Conflict to Constitutional Crisis: The Key Role of the Municipal Issue* (University of Minnesota, Minnesota Mediterranean and East European Monograph No. 8, 2001), pp. 187-88.

27

the circumstances there was no need for the creation of an army. The crisis in the government was never resolved and an army was never established as provided by the constitution. A destructive consequence of that deadlock was the emergence of underground military groups, types of "private armies," on both sides. These groups were largely controlled by aspiring political leaders who did not report to any authority. The emergence of private ethnic armies revived old fears, suspicions, and uncertainty among the two communities. Both sides began to realize that they could not rely on an inoperative state for their security and proceeded to take measures for their own protection.

In sum, the institutional framework of the Republic of Cyprus reflected the divided past and antagonistic loyalties of the two ethnic groups. The disproportional rights and privileges granted to the minority did not counterbalance the dynamics of majority-minority dynamics and relations. As Anna Jarstad points out, "although the agreements including the ethnic quota system did imply strong guarantees for ethnic rights, they were in practice insufficient for providing safety for the Turkish Cypriots. Rather, the discrepancy between formal and real power was great and the grievances increased."[26] The two communities were treated as distinct self-contained political units and political boundaries were established between them parallel to the ethnic cleavage. The political institutions of the state formalized and reinforced ethnic differences through political structures and practices. Ethnic fragmentation and political segregation of the two communities had a negative effect on the newborn republic. Political separation along ethnic lines prevented the two

---

[26] Anna Jarstad, *Changing the Game: Consociational Theory and Ethnic Quotas in Cyprus and New Zealand* (Uppsala University, Department of Peace and Conflict Research, Report No. 58, 2001), p. 165.

communities from participating and interacting in a common political arena. The coincidence of linguistic, ethnic, religious, cultural, and political cleavages eliminated any chance for cross-cutting political activities, overarching loyalties, and shared political culture supportive of the state. The two communities remained ethnically and politically distinct and looked upon each other as ethno political antagonists, without distinguishing ethnicity from politics. Rather, ethnicity dominated politics and it was natural for both sides to seek to ethnicize the state in their favor. As a result, Cypriot politics were heavily colored by ethnicity and turned into an implacable ethnic struggle, rather than a fair political game. In sum, the ethno political polarization inherited from the past, the structural inadequacies of the new state, the lack of experience in self-government, and the absence of a consensual political leadership that could transcend ethnic differences were the major factors which contributed to the generation of an open ethnic confrontation and the collapse of the Cypriot state in 1963, three years after its establishment.

Ethnic and Social Fragmentation

The legal controversies and political polarization which paralyzed the state and the political process merely created the "superstructure" of a similarly ethnically polarized and potentially explosive "infrastructure" inherited from the past. Socially, the two ethnic groups remained largely divided. The epitome of their social segregation was the absence of intermarriage and limited participation in joint social and cultural events. Greek and Turkish social activities were closely related to distinct religious beliefs and practices, ethnic holidays, and cultural traditions. Therefore, there was not enough common ground for social interaction. Intermarriage was extremely rare, since it carried with it a social and religious stigma. In effect, marriage of a Greek Orthodox with a Turkish Moslem was prohibited under the separate family laws of the two communities.

In the professional field and party organization, the two communities were largely self-sufficient and self-contained. They had separate political parties, professional organizations, and labor unions with mostly uniethnic membership. The major Greek Cypriot political parties at the time of independence were the pro-*enosis* Patriotic Front and the pro-independence communist party, AKEL. The major Turkish Cypriot parties were the Turkish Cypriot People's Party and the National Front. Both held pro-partition views. The ethnic based division of political parties was partly due to the ethno political division provided by the institutional framework of the state. The absence of common parties and organizations articulating the economic interests of the two ethnic groups across ethnic boundaries further widened the gap between the two sides.

The segregation of education inherited from the colonial era was preserved and reinforced. The two communal chambers, acting separately and in accordance with the constitution, passed legislation that to a large extent established educational unity of the two communities with their motherlands. The curricula and textbooks used in Cypriot elementary and high schools were mostly imported from the two mainlands. Ethnic and political controversies also undermined early efforts for the establishment of a badly needed university. The first state-supported University of Cyprus was established by law in 1989 and began operating in 1992. The limited communal interaction in the educational and intellectual fields sustained one-sided "ethnic ways" of thinking among the two communities. The result was a growing gap in the perceptions held by the two sides about each other.

The two communities also had their own newspapers and other publications which mostly presented biased ethnic views and conflicting positions. Besides the local press, publications imported from Greece and Turkey emphasizing Greek-Turkish antagonism enhanced mutual fears and biased perceptions.

Despite the declaration of Cypriot independence, the two communities continued celebrating the national holidays of Greece and Turkey, which were mostly directed against each other. It should be recalled that the celebration of Greek and Turkish national holidays was allowed, if not encouraged, by the constitution. These celebrations – which as a rule included pompous parades, pageants, and flying of flags – cultivated mutually negative sentiments at the grassroots level. The Greek and Turkish national anthems and flags were used during these celebrations (Cyprus has no national anthem of its own to the present day). These ethnic celebrations quite naturally reminded the people on the two sides of the ethnic line that their ethnic roots and loyalties extended to Greece and Turkey, and that the Cypriot state did not fulfill their national aspirations. As a result, any prospects for the development of a supportive political culture and mass legitimacy for the new state were undermined.

Perhaps the most destructive element in biethnic relations was the fact that the two communities failed to abandon their old conflicting ethno political goals of *enosis* and partition. This was manifested in the attitudes of the communal elites who missed no opportunity to deliver intense patriotic speeches reaffirming their continuing commitment to the achievement of those goals. In effect, the creation of an independent state was viewed by the two sides as an interim phase for materialization of *enosis* or partition.

Proposal to Revise the Constitution

Repeated ethnically colored legal and political deadlocks caused tension which led to a breakdown of the Zurich and London settlement. The political life of the Republic was polarized along ethnic lines and the state was headed for paralysis. Under these circumstances, President Makarios took the initiative for an amendment of certain articles of the constitution. In November 1963, he made a proposal of 13 points to Vice-President Kutchuk for "revision of at least some of those provisions which impede the smooth functioning and development of the State."[27] Makarios argued that a revision of the constitution was necessary because "one of the consequences of the difficulties created by certain Constitutional provisions is to prevent the Greeks and Turks of Cyprus from co-operating in a spirit of understanding and friendship, to undermine the relations between them and cause them to draw further apart instead of closer together, to the detriment of the well-being of the people of Cyprus as a whole."[28] The proposed amendment addressed mainly constitutional deadlocks. The most important of them were the following: abolition of the veto right of the president and the vice-president; abolition of the separate majority votes in the parliament; establishment of unified municipalities; unification of the administration of justice; participation of the two communities in the public service in proportion to their population; and abolition of the Greek communal chamber.

---

[27] Memorandum submitted by President Makarios to Vice-President Kutchuk on 30 November 1963 under the heading "Suggested Measures to Facilitate the Smooth Functioning of the State and Remove Certain Causes of Intercommunal Friction."

[28] Ibid.

Makarios' proposals were aimed at the establishment of a unitary state with majority rule. This would mean elimination of some of the privileges and safeguards of the minority. Vice-President Kutchuk rejected the proposals as completely unacceptable and of a sweeping nature aimed at the destruction of the Republic and attainment of *enosis*. He insisted that Cyprus should remain a bi-communal state, or complete separation of the two ethnic groups should come into effect through partition of the island.

Flare-up and Internationalization of the Problem

Constitutional crises, political immobilization, ethnic passion, mutual mistrust, suspicion, fear, uncertainty, limited bi-communal interaction, and the emergence of underground military groups paved the way for an open communal confrontation. Both communities had already begun stockpiling arms since the declaration of independence. The inevitable came in December 1963, when heavy fighting broke out in the capital city of Nicosia and soon spread to other parts of the island.

The outbreak of hostilities brought about a breakdown of intercommunal relations. A process of physical separation of the two communities began in December 1963. The Turkish Cypriots moved into armed enclaves which emerged in various parts of the island. The Turkish Cypriot leadership and public servants withdrew from the government and set up a separate administration (it was only in 1974 that the separation was completed, when the Turkish invasion of Cyprus resulted in the creation of two ethnic zones by forced movement of population).

In essence, from 1960 to 1964 the Cyprus issue went through a transformation. As James points out, "the crisis of 1963-64 changed the political character of Cyprus in a truly fundamental way."[29] The troubled colonial relationship with Britain came to an end and domestic ethnic conflict emerged as the dominant problem. After taking the form of open armed confrontation it entered a course of internationalization.

Cyprus was now an independent state and, therefore, an autonomous unit within the international system. It could pursue its own foreign policy and interact directly with other states and international organizations. The young republic sought to establish itself in the international arena by becoming a member of international organizations and establishing relations with other countries. It became a member of the United Nations, the Council of Europe, the Commonwealth of Nations, and other international organizations. It joined the Non-Aligned Movement and established diplomatic relations with several countries. Membership in the world community linked Cypriot developments to the web of international politics. Cyprus was no longer a colonial problem which could be contained within the jurisdiction of the imperial power. Outside parties could now interact directly with the new state and the parties involved in the conflict.

The complicated treaty structure by which the Cyprus Republic was bound at birth also established channels of external interference in Cypriot affairs. The treaties of establishment, alliance, and guarantee gave Britain, Greece, and Turkey the right to station forces in Cyprus and intervene, jointly or unilaterally, in Cypriot affairs. Any change of the status quo created by the London and Zurich accords could cause intervention from outside.

The power vacuum created with the British withdrawal from Cyprus was another factor conducive to the internationalization of the ethnic conflict. With the removal of British administration and the declaration of

---

[29] James (2002), p. 179.

34

independence, Cyprus became a *terra nullius* in superpower politics. Both superpowers had the interest and the means to influence developments on the island. The United States could use its junior allies – Britain, Greece, and Turkey – to influence the course of events and seek a settlement safeguarding Western interests in Cyprus. The Soviet Union could use AKEL, the powerful Greek Cypriot communist party, to influence Cypriot politics and future developments. President Makarios had already established a political alliance with AKEL and friendly relations with Moscow. The outbreak of communal hostilities presented an opportunity and a challenge to both superpowers to fish in troubled waters and promote their goals.

Ethnic ties between the two Cypriot communities and Greece and Turkey were especially instrumental in causing foreign involvement in Cypriot affairs. They provided the basis for the establishment of close relations between the two local ethnic groups and their mother countries. The Cypriots looked upon Greece and Turkey as their protectors and counted on their diplomatic, military, economic, and moral support. Greece and Turkey viewed the two Cypriot communities as parts of the Greek and Turkish nations and considered the Cyprus issue as their "national issue." Cyprus carried a heavy load of national pride and honor and had a great appeal in domestic Greek and Turkish politics. Geographic proximity and strategic considerations added another dimension to Greek and Turkish interests in Cyprus.

Attachment of the two ethnic groups to two rival states, which have been at sword's edge for centuries, prevented the generation of common patriotic bonds or overarching loyalties supportive of the newborn Cypriot state. The "suspicion syndrome" dominating Greek-Turkish relations and perceptions was transplanted into Cyprus and eliminated any hope for constructive interaction among the Cypriots. It was in this setting of national polarization and cross boundary ethnic alliances that intercommunal violence erupted in 1963. The communal flare-up provided an opportunity for the mainlands to come in support of their local ethnic groups and become involved in Cyprus and part of the Cyprus problem.

The 1967 Crisis

The already tense Greek-Turkish relations deteriorated further with the ascent to power of a Greek nationalist right-wing military junta in April 1967. Seven months later, in November, another short but sharp crisis made Cyprus a flashpoint in international politics and brought Greece and Turkey again to the brink of war. The United States urgently intervened diplomatically to manage the crisis and prevent its escalation. President Johnson hastily dispatched former Secretary of Defense Cyrus Vance to the troubled region with the succinct instruction: "Do what you have to stop the war. If you need anything let me know."[30]

The American envoy was successful in resolving the crisis by exercising pressure on the Greek military regime, which was largely responsible for the crisis, and satisfying most of the Turkish demands. Among the Turkish demands met was the withdrawal of the 10,000 Greek troops which had infiltrated into Cyprus in 1964.

Although the 1967 crisis was eventually resolved, a settlement of the broader ethno political conflict never came within sight. The US could exercise considerable influence on Greece and Turkey, but that was not enough for the promotion of a final and comprehensive solution. President Makarios, with Moscow on his side, showed no

---

[30] Quoted in Cyrus Vance, *Hard Choices: Critical Years in American Foreign Policy: Memoirs* (New York: Simon and Schuster, 1983), p. 144.

interest in negotiating such a settlement with western powers. Therefore, the problem remained and so did the prospects for another flare-up and more bloodshed.

The 1974 Crisis and Its Aftermath

The strong antipathy towards Makarios shared by Washington and the military regime in Athens provided the impetus for a new round of violence and bloodshed in 1974. Following a seven year period of tension and hostility with Makarios, the Greek military regime attempted to overthrow him. On 15 July 1974, the Greek forces stationed on Cyprus and the Greek-controlled Cypriot National Guard staged a bloody coup against the Cypriot president that brought to power an extremist pro-*enosis* puppet regime.

Turkey reacted fiercely to the military intervention of Athens by invading Cyprus and occupying 35 percent of the island. The Turkish government justified its action on legal and ethnic grounds. It argued that the Greek coup was a step toward annexation, which was prohibited by the 1960 Treaty of Guarantee. It also claimed that the Treaty of Guarantee had established a responsibility and a right for Turkey to intervene and protect the Turkish Cypriots. According to the Turkish argument, the nationalist policies and behavior of the Greek military regime posed a direct threat to the Turkish community on the island.

The coup and the invasion of 1974 once again brought Greece and Turkey to the brink of war and necessitated outside diplomatic intervention. The US, deeply concerned over the prospects of a catastrophic escalation of the crisis, offered to mediate and prevent an "unthinkable" war from happening. Secretary of State Henry Kissinger dispatched Undersecretary for Political Affairs Joseph Sisco to the troubled region two days after the coup, while Turkey was preparing for the invasion.

Sisco failed to prevent the invasion and a second diplomatic initiative was taken by Britain to contain the crisis and its consequences. A peace conference was held in Geneva under the chairmanship of the British Foreign Minister James Callaghan, but without success.

The 1974 confrontation brought to Cyprus destruction and demographic changes unique in its history. Following the diplomatic failures of Sisco and Callaghan, Turkey launched a second massive attack on Cyprus, completing its control of 35 percent of the island and bringing about an exchange of populations by force. The Greek Cypriots living in the north were forced to move to the south and the Turkish Cypriots living in the south were transferred to the north. This exchange of populations, which made one third of the Cypriots refugees in their own country, brought into effect a physical separation of the two communities that had been living together for four centuries. The forceful creation of two separate ethnic zones demarcated by the heavily fortified "Attila line" eliminated any interaction between the two sides and made the reunification of the island a difficult task.

Searching for a Settlement

Several attempts to devise a solution made so far by the UN, or in the name of the UN failed. The most recent one, which lasted four years, culminated in the submission of a comprehensive plan for a settlement (known as the Annan Plan after the UN Secretary General, Kofi Annan) in 2004, but almost immediately ended in failure. The Greek Cypriots and the Turkish Cypriots, along with Greece and Turkey, played a role in this effort. However, the United Nations in close cooperation with the European Union, the United States, and Britain also played a role and contributed in shaping the Annan Plan. The Plan was finalized by the UN Secretary General during a hasty conference in Switzerland, in March 2004, and presented to the leaders of Greece, Turkey, the Greek Cypriots, and the Turkish Cypriots. In finalizing his Plan, the UN Secretary General used his discretion "to fill in the blanks" and complete the text on issues on which the two sides failed to reach an agreement. In a way, the Plan was not exactly and fully the result of negotiation, but rather a compromise on several key issues reflecting external involvement and an urgency to overcome long-standing deadlocks and settle the problem a few days before Cyprus's accession to the EU. It provided for the establishment of a new state of affairs on the island based on a loose bi-zonal, bi-communal federal political system.[31] It was a huge text comprising a federal constitution of about 250 pages, a constitution for each of the two constituent states, and about 9,000 pages of laws for the new United Republic of Cyprus.[32]

On April 24 April 2004, the two Cypriot communities held separate, simultaneous referenda on the Annan Plan. Voters in the two communities were asked to answer "yes" or "no" to the following question: "*Do you approve the Foundation Agreement with all its Annexes, as well as the constitution of the Greek Cypriot/Turkish Cypriot State and the provisions as to the laws to be in force, to bring into being a new state of affairs in which Cyprus joins the European Union united?*"[33]

---

[31] For an extensive account on the developments which led to the shaping of the Annan Plan and its failure, see the "Report of the Secretary General on his Mission of Good Offices in Cyprus", UN doc. S/2004/437 of 28 May 2004.

[32] The Annan Plan was submitted in five versions during the period from November 2002 to April 2004. As indicated by its official title, it aimed at "The Comprehensive Settlement of the Cyprus Problem."

[33] The question was included in the Annan Plan, *Annex IX: Coming into being of the New State of Affairs*, art. 1.

A majority of the Greek Cypriots (75.8%) voted "no" and a majority of the Turkish Cypriots (64.9%) voted "yes". The Greek-Cypriot rejection of the Annan Plan evoked a negative reaction from the international community, especially the UN, the EU, the USA and Britain. As the UN Secretary General put it, it was "another missed opportunity to resolve the Cyprus problem."[34] Apparently a majority of the Greek Cypriots believed that the Plan was neither fair nor functional. In particular the provisions on security, the Turkish settlers Q9, the gradual withdrawal of the Turkish army, the exchange of properties, and the return of refugees made Greek Cypriot voters especially unhappy. There were also serious questions about the implementation and viability of the Plan, which created feelings of uncertainty and insecurity among Greek Cypriots.[35]

The results of the referenda and the accession of Cyprus to the EU a week later created a new political setting. The Greek Cypriots joined the EU, but at least temporarily lost some of the international support they had enjoyed for decades. The Turkish Cypriots and Turkey, on the other hand, gained some political benefits. Turkey, however, which started accession negotiations with the EU in 2005, continues to face difficulties in its European policy because of the Cyprus dispute.

---

[34] "Report of the Secretary General on his Mission of Good Offices in Cyprus", UN doc. S/2004/437 of 28 May 2004, p. 18.

[35] An elaborate account of the Greek Cypriot positions on the weaknesses and rejection of the Annan Plan was presented in a long letter by the President of the Republic of Cyprus to the UN Secretary General dated 7 June 2004. For an insightful analysis of the background, context and failure of the Annan Plan, see DAVID HANNAY, CYPRUS: THE SEARCH FOR A SOLUTION 1 (I.B. Tauris & Co. Ltd. 2005) (original date of publication).

Role of the European Union

Since the accession of Cyprus on 1 May 2004, the EU, in cooperation with the United Nations, has been in a unique position to play a role on Cyprus and in the region. The parties involved are either part of the EU or have special relations with it and can, therefore, appreciate and support a European contribution or initiative on Cyprus. Greece is a member-state while Turkey is as close to the EU as a nonmember-state can be, following the commencement of accession negotiations. Britain, a major partner in the EU and a guarantor power of the independence and unity of Cyprus under the 1960 settlement of the colonial issue, is in a privileged position to play a constructive role within and outside the EU context. The United States is also concerned with Cyprus because the Eastern Mediterranean is a region of vital geopolitical importance to it, Turkey is an "important strategic partner", and Greece is an "old good friend".

The EU favors a settlement that will reunite the island and its people under a bi-zonal bi-communal federation. Such a solution would, of course, have to guarantee the civil, political, economic and cultural rights of all Cypriots without any restriction or discrimination, and the security of all Cypriots in each and every respect – and not only in military terms. The institutions, legal order, principles and policies of the EU – the *acquis communautaire* – have the capacity to provide a conducive framework in the search for a solution on Cyprus. A settlement based on the law, policies and practices of the EU could provide a sound basis for peaceful coexistence and prosperity for all Cypriots, given the role of the European integration process, for half a century, in bringing states and peoples together under conditions of interdependence and peaceful co-existence. The dynamics of the single market and the advent of economic and

41

monetary union have taken over in strengthening the conditions for peace, as the free movement of people, goods, services and capital reduces the risks of intercommunal conflict.

Under the circumstances, it is not surprising that the most widely canvassed settlement is one based on a bi-zonal and bi-communal form of federation where all citizens would enjoy universally accepted rights and opportunities all over the island. Given the realities of Cyprus – geography, economy, size, distribution of natural resources, demography, and the political failures of the past – a federal solution seems to be the only pragmatic way out of the stalemate.

Looking at the broader impact that European integration may have on the triangle of Cyprus, Turkey and Greece, it could be argued that the EU provides a new context within which the relations of the three countries can improve. In recent years, Greek-Turkish relations have improved considerably and Greece's policy towards Turkish accession is a positive one, but this cannot always be taken for granted as it depends on the political barometer in Europe as well as over the Aegean and Cyprus. The fact that Turkey does not recognize the Republic of Cyprus – a full member of the EU – may lead to political complications, especially in the context of accession negotiations, but by resolving the Cyprus problem Turkey can expect major political benefits from Europe.

Conclusion

In general, a settlement of the Cyprus problem may have a catalytic effect on Greek-Turkish relations and generate a momentum for addressing other bilateral issues. Moreover, it cannot go unnoticed that Cyprus has not only been a source of Greek-Turkish tension, but also a major economic burden for the two countries that traditionally included the island in their defense doctrines and strategies. For Turkey, the burden is much higher because it maintains a sizable army on the island (about 30,000 troops) and also provides extensive financial support to the Turkish Cypriots. The failures of the Annan Plan, the accession of Cyprus, and the ongoing accession negotiations between Turkey and the EU, have created a new reality, additional urgency and a promising prospect. A new momentum is needed for the reunification of the island, which is too small to remain divided but big enough to accommodate its entire people as a reunited EU member-state.

I

CYPRUS REUNIFICATION: TIME FOR TRACK III DIPLOMACY[36]

Introduction

My experience as a Fulbright Senior Scholar in conflict resolution on the eastern Mediterranean island of Cyprus, and the failure of the United Nations (UN) efforts to achieve reunification of the Greek Cypriot and Turkish Cypriot communities in conflict there, provide a classic example of the need for reconfiguration of the struggle for universal peace. As the world becomes smaller through the advent of social networks, it is clear there must be such a reconfiguration. The extreme sacrifice of life, liberty, property, and social institutions resulting from the refusal of the elite practice of diplomacy to recognize the needs of abused people, severe violations of human rights, ethnic divisions, and the right of all people to determine their own destinies, seem to be ignored world-wide on a daily basis.

In 1960 the island of Cyprus achieved its independence from England. By 1963 the Greek Cypriot majority was engaged in the ethnic cleansing of the Turkish Cypriot minority. This was reversed in 1974 when 30,000-35,000 Turkish troops arrived on the northern part of the island to engage in the same conduct. The troops' presence eventually resulted in the partition and creation of the breakaway "Turkish Republic of Northern Cyprus," recognized by no country in the world other than Turkey.

---

[36] *See* A. Marco Turk. 2006. "Cyprus Reunification is Long Overdue: The Time is Right for Track III Diplomacy as the Best Approach for Successful Negotiation of This Ethnic Conflict." *LOY. L.A. INT'L & COMP. L. REV.* 28:205-255.

Depending on the particular point of view, Turkey either *invaded* the island to *occupy* the northern part, or was *forced* by international inaction to send troops to *protect* the Turkish Cypriot minority from potential additional abuse by the Greek Cypriot majority.[37] Notwithstanding UN efforts since 1974 to reestablish a central government and obtain the agreement of both communities to live together peacefully on the island, the conflict remains intractable and ripe for Track III (grassroots) intervention to achieve a reconfiguration.

According to Joseph S. Joseph, the "Cyprus problem" (which, unless it is included as part of quoted material, I prefer to refer to as the *Cyprus Problem* because it is in fact a state of being) is a domestic ethnic conflict with international overtones because it involves parties within a single state identifiable by characteristics (e.g., geographic region, ideology, language, religion, or ethnicity).[38] Adding to the mix is Turkey's continued occupation of approximately 37 percent of the island with its troops, ignoring repeated UN attempts to require withdrawal of all foreign troops from Cyprus in an effort to guarantee the island's sovereignty and territorial integrity.[39] The most recent and seemingly concentrated attempts to resolve the Cyprus problem were the five versions of the plan proposed by UN Secretary-General Kofi Annan (Annan I, II, III, IV, and V) between

---

[37] *See* HANNAY, *supra* note 35, at 5-7.

[38] *See* JOSEPH S. JOSEPH, CYPRUS: ETHNIC CONFLICT AND INTERNATIONAL POLITICS (FROM INDEPENDENCE TO THE THRESHOLD OF THE EUROPEAN UNION 4, 37-39, 45 (Palgrave Macmillan, 2d ed. 1997).

[39] *See also* CLAIRE PALLEY, AN INTERNATIONAL RELATIONS DEBACLE: THE UN SECRETARY-GENERAL'S MISSION OF GOOD OFFICES IN CYPRUS 1999-2004, 15 (Hart Publishing UK 2005).

October 2002 and March 2004 that were rejected, thus failing to accomplish their purpose. Without fanfare, these efforts had been doomed to fail because, on December 13, 2002, the EU, although still hoping for a reunited island by the time the Accession Treaty would be signed, relaxed its reunification requirements for Cyprus and accepted the candidacy for accession of a divided island. The stick had been removed leaving only the carrot.[40]

Key Points in Five Versions of Annan Plan

Annan I[41]

A new common state of Cyprus was created with its own constitution (each component state could draft its own so long as it would not be incompatible with the overall settlement). Numerous annexes dealt with, among other things, security, property, territorial adjustment, and European Union (EU) issues. If both Greek Cypriot and Turkish Cypriot community-approval referendum vote results were positive, the set of agreements would become effective the following day, so that the EU could take appropriate action to admit to membership the new unified Cyprus. With respect to status, sovereignty, and continuity, there would be a "new state of affairs in Cyprus" referred to as "Cyprus" or the "State of Cyprus." The result would be a "single international legal personality" consisting of two separate states. The "common state" would exercise the constitutional powers allocated to it while the component states would exercise all other powers. There would be no hierarchy between the two levels.

All prior acts of the Greek Cypriot Republic of Cyprus and the Turkish Cypriot TRNC would be

---

[40] *See ibid.* at 275, Appendix 6. See also HANNAY, supra note 35, at 192, 194-195.

[41] *See* HANNAY, *supra* note 35, at 182-185.

46

legitimized so long as they did not contradict the settlement terms. The new "state of affairs" (*not* "state") would be "indissoluble" so that neither secession nor domination of any other institution by one side would be possible. Foreign affairs, EU relations, central-bank functions, common-state finances (to the extent relevant), economic and trade policy, aviation and navigation policy, as well as some more technical matters, were allocated to the common state. The Swiss model for an executive council of the common state was followed (four Greek Cypriots and two Turkish Cypriots chosen be each side, respectively) requiring agreement by at least one member from each side. The council would select a president and vice-president from among its members, rotating every six months with never less than a 2:1 rotation. However, for the first 36 months of the new state of affairs the two leaders (Glafcos Clerides for the Greek Cypriots and Rauf Denktash for the Turkish Cypriots) would serve as "co-presidents."

Two houses of parliament would be established for the common state: The upper house would be divided 50:50 between Greek Cypriots and Turkish Cypriots elected by the legislatures of their respective component states. The lower house would be elected by popular vote, and the share of seats could not be less than 25 percent for either side. No legislation could be passed without approval of both houses, and Turkish Cypriots were protected from subornation of any of their members during any effort to pass anti-Turkish Cypriot legislation. To avoid the possibility of a deadlock, and to permit it to break ties in the event other institutions deadlocked, a supreme court would be comprised of three Greek Cypriots, three Turkish Cypriots, and three non-Cypriots. Regarding security, neither of the two separate states could secede nor unite with any outside state.

The number of Greek Cypriot and Turkish Cypriot troops that could remain on the island was limited (somewhere between 1,000 and 9,999). Disbanding of all Cypriot forces with removal of arms, a legally binding arms embargo, and island-wide UN-mandated international military presence for an indefinite period was prescribed. Territorial adjustment providing for transfer of additional property to Greek Cypriots, enabling the return of more Greek Cypriots and displacement of fewer Turkish Cypriots, was specified. A "property board" was to be established to handle mutual compensation for lost property and determination of "right of residence." A moratorium on return was to exist for three years regarding unoccupied property and five years for occupied property. While no decision was made regarding Turkish Cypriot citizenship for post-1974 Turkish immigrants, all Cypriots would be Cypriot citizens as well as citizens of their respective component states. *Settlement of the Cyprus Problem and EU membership were inseparable.* Rights of establishment and purchase of property were restricted. Cyprus's military participation in EU Security and Defense Policy was ruled out. EU financial assistance would be sought to narrow the economic gap between Greek Cypriots and Turkish Cypriots. And a reconciliation commission was proposed to facilitate healing of wounds and to deal with "antagonistic interpretations of historical events."

Annan II[42]

The main changes to Annan I were in the areas of political citizenship, the transitional presidency, and the residual presence of Greek and Turkish troops. Political citizenship could be held in only one component state or the other, not both; and a four-year moratorium would be imposed on Greek Cypriots moving to the north and Turkish Cypriots moving to the south, with caps established regarding such change in residencies. The

---

[42]*See Ibid.* at 189-191.

48

definition of Cypriot citizenship was revised so that, in effect, most Turkish immigrants (even post-1974) would become citizens of the Turkish Cypriot component state, and provision was made for EU financial assistance to those who were refused permanent residency and were repatriated. Further territorial map adjustments were made, and a cap was placed on property restitution. A "relocation board" was proposed to help displaced persons resulting from territorial adjustments, including direct UN involvement. The transitional presidency of the two signatory co-presidents of the component state (Clerides and Denktash) was reduced from three years to 30 months. There could be no amendment of the basic articles of the new constitution, and the European Parliament seats allocated to Cyprus would be divided two-thirds Greek Cypriot and one-third Turkish Cypriot. Management of natural resources would become a common rather than component state responsibility, and EU safeguard measures to protect the Turkish Cypriot component state were increased. The residual presence of Greek and Turkish troops was specified to be 2,500-7,500, and it was left to Greece and Turkey to negotiate the actual figure. The two component states, as well as Greece and Turkey, would need to consent to any international military operation in the "new" Cyprus, and the required notice to the UN concerning troop movements of the residual contingent forces remaining on the island was raised.

Annan III[43]

The decision was made to submit the proposed settlement plan for approval at separate simultaneous referenda in each community; effectively taking the two leaders "off the hook" so their only obligation would be to put the proposal to their respective voters. If both

---

[43] *See Ibid.* at 208-211.

electorates approved the proposal, the two leaders would be bound (along with Greece, Turkey, and Britain, the three guarantor powers) to put the voter-approved plan into operation the next day. (*However, I believe the death knell to reunification occurred when it was made clear that a negative vote on the referenda would not invalidate EU accession.*) Cyprus would be renamed "The United Cyprus Republic," an "independent and sovereign state with a single international legal personality, and a federal government" consisting of "two constituent states, namely the Greek Cypriot State and the Turkish Cypriot State." Annan III increased Turkish Cypriot land to 29.2 percent. The two constituent states would each gain the right to determine their own internal citizenship. Annan III increased the moratorium on the Greek Cypriot right of residence in the north to six years and adjusted the length of the various periods following expiration of the moratorium. When Turkey would accede to EU membership, all remaining Greek and Turkish troops would be removed from Cyprus. In the meantime, it would no longer be required that Greece and Turkey agree to international military operations on the island. Restriction was imposed on the definition of the term "religious sites" so as to prevent the Greek Cypriot Orthodox Church from excessive repossession of property in the north. A specific list of 45,000 Turkish immigrants who would have the right to Turkish Cypriot citizenship was advanced. Exemption of students and academic staff from residency limitations and immigration controls was provided.

Most favored nation status was included for Turkey. Debts were to be assumed by the respective constituent states. Six thousand Turkish and Greek troops were permitted to remain on the island. However, the advance notice required for ordinary troop movements would be reduced to two days, and to three days for troop exercises. The EU and the Council of Europe would endorse the settlement so as to avoid property litigation. The new federal government would harmonize the economies of the two constituent states. The EU would be requested to convene a "donor conference" to raise funds for displacement costs resulting from territorial and other adjustments. The increase in territorial adjustments and overall property reinstatement limits favored Greek Cypriots. An unlimited number of Greek Cypriots could return to certain specified villages that would have the sole responsibility for their own cultural and educational affairs. Greek Cypriots residing in the Turkish Cypriot constituent state would have immediate voting rights in European and local elections. Greek Cypriots over the age of 65 would have only a two-year moratorium regarding their return to property in the north, and all quantitative restrictions would be removed. Nine years permanent residence would be a prerequisite to attaining Cypriot citizenship. Non-Cypriot supreme court judges would only be permitted to have a voice if Cypriots could not agree, and a "Court of First Instance" would be created. Rules regarding entry and residence rights would need to be compatible with the Schengen agreement.[44] Resolution of the missing-persons issue from 1974 would be given constitutional force. Annan III also covered removal of Greek and Turkish troops from the island, elimination of the requirement that Greece and Turkey agree to international military operations, and removal of limits on Greek Cypriot residence in the north, upon Turkey's accession to the EU.

---

[44] The 1985 agreement between France, Germany, Belgium, Luxembourg and the Netherlands, signed at Schengen, Luxembourg, providing for the end of controls on their common internal borders so that a single external border for immigration checks was established with one set of rules. Explanation available at http://europa.eu.int/scadplus/leg/en/lvb/133020.htm.

Annan IV and V[45]

In early February 2004, the parties agreed to resume negotiations "under the aegis of the UN and on the basis of the Annan Plan," with the Greek and Turkish governments joining in if necessary. If this failed, Annan would prepare and submit a new version of his plan for voter approval (during the April 24, 2004 referendum elections). In the meantime, EU draft legislation for a reunited Cyprus would be completed. Because Annan failed to obtain agreement on amendments (Annan IV) to earlier versions of his plan, he was forced to abandon a final definitive version of his plan (Annan V). However, it was Annan V (although not fundamentally different from earlier versions) that was submitted to the Greek Cypriot and Turkish Cypriot voters on April 24, 2004. The poll results demonstrated that rational self-interest was necessary to overcome the "demons of history and prejudice," something that was not possible here given the elitist Track I (leaders only) approach taken from the very beginning. Although purportedly the Turkish Cypriot leader Rauf Denktash had publicly referred to the Annan Plan as "dead and off the table," the widespread opinion of the international community was that it was "the most sophisticated and the most complete attempt ever made" to solve the Cyprus Problem, and that EU membership by a reunited Cyprus was "the keystone of any settlement." Apparently, the Turkish Cypriots who voted "yes" (approximately65%) agreed, but the Greek Cypriots voting "no" (approximately 75%) did not. After more than one thousand years, Nicosia, the capital of Cyprus, maintains its distinction as the only militarily divided city in Europe.[46] At least for the

---

[45] *See* HANNAY, *supra* note 35, at 241-246.

[46] Explanation *available at* http://www.cosmosnet.net/azias/cyprus/nicosia.html.

immediate future, it will remain so along with the entire island.

Approach Shaped by Ethnic-Political Dynamic[47]

If we are to appreciate the unique attributes of this ethnic conflict, we must consider the historical chain of events that mixed religion, culture and politics as a powerful dynamic in the years when attempts at resolution took place. The history of the conflict is a weight that bears heavily on those who sit at the negotiating table. Historically, outside powers have dominated the island and its politics, causing both communities to tend to defer to interlopers in determining their fate. The British have not been trusted or liked by either side, especially when many have felt Britain's decision to abandon efforts to resolve the problem and instead leave it to the Cypriots for resolution, while at the same time establishing two Sovereign Base Areas for themselves, indicated a willingness to look the other way that encouraged hard line positions on both sides of the conflict. Archbishop Makarios, as President of the Republic of Cyprus, openly expressed an opinion that independence would lead to enosis, and neither Greece nor Turkey did much to help make the bi-communal aspect of independence succeed. The United States' interest has primarily been to strategically avoid open hostilities between Greece and Turkey that would weaken NATO, while the former Soviet Union provided unquestioning support to Makarios in an effort to do just the opposite. Enosis and *taksim* (seeing that the northern part of the island becomes part of Turkey as a result of partition or "double enosis") reared their nationalistic heads periodically throughout the history of the conflict. Three international treaties between Greece, Turkey and the United Kingdom negatively affected exercise of its

---

[47] *See* HANNAY, *supra* note 35, at 1-9, 241.

sovereignty by Cyprus (the Treaty of Guaranty prevented secession or Cypriot unification with any other state; the Treaty of Alliance permitted a small joint military force composed of Greek and Turkish troops on the island; and the Treaty of Establishment granted the United Kingdom its sovereignty over the 99 square miles comprising the two Sovereign Base Areas).

The United Nations has been unable to do much to improve the security situation on the island since 1964 when it first deployed its initial small military force. Had it not been for the forceful intervention by then President Lyndon B. Johnson in 1967, Turkish troops would have arrived on the island as part of a military intervention force. Since 1963, and especially following the Turkish intervention of 1974, with the exception of Turkey, the UN and the rest of the international community has treated the Greek Cypriots as the sole legitimate government of Cyprus. During his lifetime, former Turkish Cypriot leader Rauf Denktash continued to argue that there could be no solution to the Cyprus Problem until that attitude was reversed (i.e., either withdrawing recognition of the Greek Cypriots or recognizing the Turkish Cypriots on an equal but separate basis).[48] In the aftermath of Turkey's hostile intervention of 1974, the ethnic cleansing was "regularized" by a 1975 agreement acknowledging the population exchange without legal recognition. While a few Greek Cypriots remain in the north and still fewer Turkish Cypriots remain in the south, the current geopolitical configuration of the island was established in 1975. Thus effectively there are two separate states, each with its own

---

[48] *Ibid.* But see Turkish Cypriots Elect New President, L.A. TIMES (California), Apr. 18, 2005, at A6 (on April 17, 2005, Mehmet Ali Talat, a pro-unification candidate, became the newly elected Turkish Cypriot leader. He immediately called for reunification and EU membership for Turkish Cypriots.).

ethnicity, separated only by a buffer zone maintained by UN peacekeeping troops.

Because Greek Cypriots have never forgotten the loss of one-third of their country (rich agricultural and commercially tourist-friendly land), they are determined to reclaim it. Compensation for this loss has been an unacceptable alternative in any settlement discussions. Greek military capability has been no match for the superior Turkish military establishment just forty miles away (not to mention the large contingent of Turkish troops already occupying the northern part of the island). So Turkish Cypriots have come to believe that they can only rely on Turkey, and are convinced that the Greek Cypriots will expel all Turkish Cypriots from the island if given the opportunity. This means that Greek Cypriots must now deal with their own security concerns as well as those of the Turkish Cypriots. Although the outsiders have been convinced of the need to work through the UN for a settlement of the Cyprus Problem, they have religiously avoided direct involvement. Subsequent efforts to achieve a settlement have concentrated on a bi-communal, bi-zonal federation framework for a solution. Obstinate machinations on the part of both sides over the ensuing years have served to frustrate any meaningful discussions for a successful settlement of the conflict.

The 1983 unilateral declaration of independence expressed by Turkey and the Turkish Cypriots, that henceforth the northern part of the island would be known as the "Turkish Republic of Northern Cyprus (TRNC)," caused the UN Security Council to issue a condemnation and called on UN members not to recognize the TRNC. None did except Turkey. The creation of the TRNC has continued to make settlement less and less attainable. This has also caused far-ranging problems for the TRNC and its attempt to participate on the international stage, widening the gap between the economies of the two communities requiring increasing dependence of Turkish Cypriots on subsidies from Turkey. The 1990 application of the Republic of Cyprus (controlled by Greek Cypriots) to become a member of the European Union was accepted as valid in 1995. However, the Turkish Cypriots subsequently refused the offer from the Greek Cypriots to become members of the Cyprus EU negotiating team. On May 1, 2004, the Greek Cypriot Republic of Cyprus alone became a member of the EU. The long-held hope that EU accession negotiations would enhance the opportunity for a resolution of the Cyprus Problem became another failure in the extensive list of dead-end attempts at settlement.

Positive Example of Track III Effectiveness

Diplomacy is a key factor in the peacebuilding process. It is practiced at three levels: Tracks I, II, and III. Track I involves individuals from the political and military elite. They influence the process at the high level of official and coercive action as well as non-coercive activities such as facilitation and negotiation. Track II involves unofficial or informal interaction between members of adversarial groups who seek to influence the process through change of public opinion, as well as utilization of organized material and human resources in an effort to achieve resolution of a conflict. Participants at the Track II level are NGOs, businesses, local and religious leaders, and ordinary citizens. This level can be effective as a connector between Tracks I and III. Finally, Track III advocates are "community-based." They employ various approaches to peaceful resolution such as public education, citizen advocacy, and events like conferences and workshops, in the attempt to "achieve reconciliation, healing, problem solving and mediation at the grassroots level." At the Track III level the effort is to encourage "multi-stakeholder dialogue, reconciliation exercises and co-existence among communities."[49]

Prior to August 1997, the civil society in Cyprus had apparently not been exposed to mediation skills and techniques. The general population on both sides received me with great enthusiasm. The response from the political elite was patronizing at best. The question to be addressed was how to empower both sides to interact with each other so as to express their respective interests and underlying needs while at the same time encouraging each to recognize, understand, and consider the other's point of view, in order to achieve resolution of conflict. I introduced three models: (1) traditional problem solving,[50] (2) transformation of relationships,[51] and (3) the humanistic-transformative[52] (that seeks to educate and establish reasonable expectations on the part of both sides to a conflict). The personal histories of murder, rape, and the missing, as well as loss of valuable property, on both sides, were something that none of the bi-communal participants

---

[49] *See* Foundation for Co-Existence (FCE): Promoting Coexistence Through Human Security, http://www.fcoex.com/pages/glossary.htm (last visited Sept. 1, 2005). There are varying opinions regarding the estimated number of tracks. *See, e.g.,* LOUISE DIAMOND & JOHN W. MCDONALD, MULTI-TRACK DIPLOMACY: A SYSTEMS APPROACH TO PEACE 1-5 (3rd ed. 1996). However, for efficient application, generally the use of three tracks is preferred.

[50] *See* generally CHRISTOPHER MOORE, THE MEDIATION PROCESS: PRACTICAL STRATEGIES FOR RESOLVING CONFLICT (Jossey-Bass: A Wiley Imprint 2003).

[51] *See* ROBERT A. BARUCH BUSH & JOSEPH P. FOLGER, THE PROMISE OF MEDIATION: RESPONDING TO CONFLICT THROUGH EMPOWERMENT AND RECOGNITION 12 (Jossey-Bass Inc. 1994). A second edition has since been published.

[52] *See* Mark S. Umbreit, Humanistic Mediation: A Transformative Journey of Peace making, 14 MEDIATION Q. 201-213 (1997).

were prepared to discuss directly with each other face-to-face, except from the vantage of leveling charges against the other community. It was easier to keep the real hurt to oneself. Consequently, the training allowed participants on each side to keep their deepest feelings buried and permitted them bi-communally to venture only so far as they were willing to go.

From 1997-1999, I trained segments of the island's Greek and Turkish Cypriot divided population in methods designed to resolve their historical conflicts. While I was acutely aware of the religious, ethnic and political conflicts to be considered in any effort to establish peacebuilding protocols, I was careful to tread lightly in these areas. By the time I left the island in 1999, I had been responsible for future establishment of a mediation center in each community. In addition I trained a bi-communal cross-section of students, teachers, administrators, doctors, lawyers, judges, social workers, mental health professionals, government employees, law enforcement and military personnel in communication skills and the three then existing approaches to mediation. The training took place over approximately five hundred hours, and was delivered to more than six hundred participants. During the last six months of 1998, I organized and worked with a group of fifty-two Cypriots comprising the "Oslo Group." These were lawyers, accountants, mental health professionals, government employees, business operators, teachers, students, media, and ordinary citizens totaling 25 from each side, plus one Greek Cypriot and one Turkish Cypriot program representative from the Cyprus Fulbright Commission. This accounts for the description of 26 citizens from each community.

The name of the group originated from their meeting in Oslo, Norway, under the auspices of the Cyprus Fulbright Commission in cooperation with the International Peace Research Institute, Oslo (PRIO), between June 29 and July 5, 1998, where the twenty-six Greek Cypriots and twenty-six Turkish Cypriots convened to participate in a conflict intervention skills training workshop for peacebuilding in Cyprus. Connecting and communicating skills were emphasized. Examples include body language; codes we establish; sharing feelings and ideas; hearing, seeing, understanding; conversational style; framing and reframing; messages and meta-messages; effect of our words and how to adjust content so we say what we mean; improving talk to improve relationships; vocal signals; power and solidarity; empathy; "stepping into each other's shoes;" reading faces and expressions; feedback; roles; ideology of communication; "tricks people play;" empowerment; willingness to listen and consider the other party's point of view; respect; forgiveness and reconciliation.[53]

Oslo was selected as the site for the workshop because the political situation on Cyprus prevented Greek and Turkish Cypriots from openly meeting together on the island. In December 1997, I was present on the island when Turkish Cypriot leader Rauf Denktash ordered the "Green Line" (the buffer zone separating the two communities guarded by UN peacekeeping troops) closed, preventing Greek Cypriots going to the north and Turkish Cypriots going to the south, as well as Turkish Cypriots entering that restricted area to participate in bi-communal events at the Fulbright Center located there, without prior TRNC approval. The training was conducted over a three-day period followed by two days of group deliberations, brainstorming their ideas for a solution to the Cyprus Problem through a bi-communal, bi-zonal federation. During these deliberations the group designated over 30

---

[53] *See* generally DEBORAH TANNEN, THAT'S NOT WHAT I MEANT: HOW CONVERSATIONAL STYLE MAKES OR BREAKS RELATIONSHIPS (1987).

possible issues to be considered, deciding on six for immediate consideration and subsequent development. These issues were: (1) Bi-communal Movement; (2) Structure of Government; (3) Security; (4) Human Rights; (5) Social Issues; and (6) Economic Issues. The issue-selection process was followed by the election of a bi-communal steering committee consisting of five members from each community plus their Cyprus Fulbright Commission representative. The meeting (Oslo I) was concluded with the issuance of a declaration by the group (Appendix A) concerning their views on the Cyprus Problem and how they hoped to contribute to a peaceful solution on the island.

Upon their return to Cyprus, the 52 members of the Oslo Group were divided into six subgroups, each containing two sections (one from each community), with each section being chaired by a steering committee member from the appropriate community. Each subgroup was assigned one of the six issues designated by the group in Oslo, and each section of that subgroup was given the assignment of preparing a draft of the particular issue under consideration by their subgroup. It was made clear to me by several members of the group at the conclusion of the workshop during evaluation that, had they not participated in the intensive three-day conflict intervention skills portion, the results would not have developed as they did.

Monthly (July-December 1998), the steering committee met bi-communally on the island for the purpose of exchanging drafts with their subgroup counterparts on the assigned issues and continued to rework the papers. These meetings took place in a restaurant located in the southern part of the island outside the small village of Pyla (a historic bi-communal village where Greek and Turkish Cypriots have lived together in peaceful harmony) in the Pergamos region on the site of the British Sovereign Base Areas very close to a Turkish Cypriot checkpoint permitting only limited passage (person and time) solely by Turkish Cypriots. Some months earlier, in the company of Greek Cypriot international human rights lawyer and friend, Achilleas Demetriades, I had discovered this limited area that is located approximately 45 minutes southeast of the capitol city of Nicosia. The meetings were able to take place because of the sympathetic owners of the restaurant. Subsequently, until April 21, 2003, when Denktash announced the lifting of all restrictions on the Green Line,[54] an increasing number of bi-communal groups adopted that approach and gravitated to the restaurant for meetings on a regular basis. Final working drafts were exchanged, and unified resulting papers were prepared for presentation to the overall group at their next meeting in Oslo.

Under the continuing auspices of the Cyprus Fulbright Commission in cooperation with PRIO, 31 members of the Oslo Group returned to Norway, from December 7-11, 1998, to consider, discuss, amend, and adopt final detailed statements of interest concerning each of the six issues. Subsequent to completion of their working sessions, the members of Oslo II were invited by PRIO to attend the one-hour live taping of the CNN interview of the two 1998 Nobel Peace Laureates, which took place at the Oslo City Hall, the site of the actual awards. After having adopted what I believe was the first expression at any track of concrete suggestions concerning issues involved in a potential Cypriot bi-communal, bi-zonal federation, this was a very moving concluding experience for all members of the group who heard the two laureates speak of forgiveness and reconciliation in Northern Ireland.

The work product of the Oslo Group was in no way intended to be exclusive, preemptive, or the only approach to the subject matter. This was simply the work of 31

---

[54] See HANNAY, *supra* note 35, at 225

61

participants at Oslo II[55] who drew upon the efforts of the 52 original members of Oslo I, to express their own collective personal interests based on their underlying needs. Though they expressed strong feelings during the negotiation process that lasted into the early hours of their last full morning in Oslo, there was no acrimony, common courtesy prevailed, and the participants gave recognition to each other through a democratic process.[56] *They acted solely as private citizens and did not claim to speak for others, officially or unofficially.* They desired only that others may consider and frankly discuss the issue of peace in Cyprus and a lasting solution to the Cyprus Problem, and that people in both communities would speak and listen to each other, practicing empowerment and recognition. They operated under the belief that the only opinions not heard are those not expressed.

These 31 dedicated people, along with their remaining 21 colleagues, intended to continue their work on these and other issues in the future, and they welcomed others to join and fully participate with them in the effort to achieve peace on the island, for the benefit and well-being of all Cypriots. They demonstrated that the results were not as important as the process employed. They could all work together and triumph over adversity, setting an example of peaceful cooperation. In this spirit, the final vote on each issue was set forth on the section divider of the report that preceded the particular presentation. The Cyprus Fulbright Commission and the U.S.-Norway Fulbright Foundation for Educational Exchange cooperated to provide this opportunity for bi-communal self-

---

[55] There were 15 Greek Cypriots and 16 Turkish Cypriots. Because of attrition due to illness, employment demands, or pre-existing personal commitments, it was not possible for all 52 original members to attend the Oslo II meeting.

[56] "Recognition" simply meant respecting differing opinions.

expression. It appears that this may have been the first such collaboration between Fulbright organizations from different countries. The Royal Norwegian Ministry of Foreign Affairs and PRIO supported this cooperative effort financially and otherwise.

In originally organizing the Oslo Group and training them in various conflict intervention skills as well as facilitating their deliberations during both meetings, and at the numerous bi-communal steering committee gatherings, I became more convinced at each stage that, if the people of this island could be left alone to work together as Cypriots without interference, they would find the solution to the problem and a lasting peace could finally be achieved in Cyprus. The fact that the members of the Oslo Group were willing to meet and work together as *private citizens* to arrive at a solution to be recommended to others, and that they actually *did succeed in doing so, is far more important than what they actually recommended.* Nevertheless, it is informative to see what they accomplished in the process, especially when comparing their success at the level of Track III diplomacy with the historical failures of the elite diplomats in Track I and the series of NGOs from Track II.

I made return trips in 2000, 2001, 2003, 2005, and 2008 to continue my peacebuilding work with both Greek and Turkish Cypriots. My peacebuilding efforts have also taken me to Norway, Israel, Turkey, and England, as well as to both coasts of the United States. In October 2003, I participated as one of only two Americans invited to attend the Oxford University international workshop on "Getting to Yes" regarding efforts to reunify Cyprus. As part of my continuing work with the Cyprus Fulbright Commission through the US State Department, I conducted a two-week education/training program for six Cypriot family court judges (three Greek and three Turkish) in the Los Angeles area in August 2004, dealing with family law in a federal system. My two earlier Fulbright/State Department

63

programs in the USA for Cypriots (lawyers, judges, law professors, and police) dealt with: (1) the administration of justice, and (2) community policing, in the United States.

The Oslo Report

The lengthy Final Report of the Oslo Group, dated December 11, 1998, is a collection of six papers, each addressing one of the following six issues designated for immediate consideration and development: Bi-communal Movement, Structure of Government, Human Rights, Social Issues, Security Issues, and Economic Issues.[57]

Bi-communal Movement[58]

The importance of the bi-communal movement is its link between the two communities. It formed a bridge between the current problem and the envisaged solution, through "cooperation, collaboration, trust and understanding between the two communities" and the exploration and examination of "common grounds on certain issues . . . regarding the envisaged solution." Its mission was to "contribute towards the establishment of a lasting peaceful Federal State" that would "safeguard the peaceful coexistence" of each community "through strong security measures in every aspect and to form one identity."

In order to be successful, the bi-communal movement would need to be institutionalized, structured, and encourage new participation through a "democratic institution whose operations will be safeguarded by democratic procedures." Detailed provisions were proposed regarding objectives, institutionalization, methods, organizational structure, a bi-communal council and

---

[57] On file with the author and also with various individuals including members of the Oslo Group, the Cyprus Fulbright Commission, officials from both communities, and the press.

[58] Adopted unanimously.

64

selection procedure with equal community membership from each bi-communal activity group, a steering committee and selection procedure for five members from each community, responsibilities for the council and steering committee, administration and accounting procedures, reference materials, and a proposed action plan.

Structure of Government[59]

A bi-communal, bi-zonal "Federal Republic of Cyprus (FRC)" would be established with "one international personality and one citizenship," consisting of "two federated states" administered respectively by each of the communities. Each of the states would be administered "on the basis of political equality in the federal structure" (legislature, executive and judiciary) with the federal constitution recognizing "all human rights of all Cypriots and shall provide for their implementation." Each state was to have its own constitution, legislative body, executive, and judiciary, and decide all issues not reserved to the federal government. The federal constitution was to be the "supreme law of the FRC" and would prevail as between the states in the event of conflict. Some of the listed powers (e.g., police) could be exercised concurrently with the federal government.

The powers of the federal legislature and executive were: foreign affairs; defense; citizenship and immigration; federal budget and federal taxation (fiscal and monetary policy and central bank); customs; federal police; port; air traffic control and civil aviation; external commerce; ensuring free and unfettered interstate trade; health; environment; natural resources; federal postal and

---

[59] Approved: 29, disapproved: 2. Both disapprovals were from Greek Cypriots. One objected to the provisions concerning sovereignty, political equality, the term "state," single chamber federal legislature, election of the president and vice-president. The other objected to the provision concerning a single chamber federal legislature.

communications services; registration of patents and trademarks; registration of companies; and any other powers that would be agreed upon by the two federated states.

The federal legislature was to be "single chamber" and consist of an "equal number of representatives of each federated state." Only "a simple majority" would be required to enact legislation. The "presidential system" was adopted for the federal government, with a vice-president to be from a different community than the president. Selection of the president was left open between election "by universal suffrage" and rotation between the two communities after election.

Flags, federal anthem, and public holidays were categories left to be decided. The proposed court system was elaborate; it provided for a lower and higher court in each state, a federal court, and the European Court of Human Rights. In some situations, a citizen could apply directly to the federal court, which was to be composed of an equal number of judges from each community. Cyprus laws would be considered in all the courts, but only the states would have jurisdiction over family law.

Human Rights[60]

Human rights were to be "approached from the point of view of the needs of every individual and must be based on international norms and criteria." It was specifically noted that these issues must be considered "in order to achieve serious progress towards the final and lasting solution." The main issues addressed are: missing persons, settlers, refugees and property, freedom of movement, and identity.

---

[60] Adopted unanimously, although one Greek Cypriot "expressed reservations as to the provisions concerning missing persons and settlers."

66

Missing Persons

This issue was to be given priority, removed from the political arena in order to avoid political exploitation, and put "into a common humanitarian perspective." Both sides encouraged continuation of the work of the "existing independent commission on missing persons," and it was suggested that representatives of the families of missing persons be involved in the efforts. Specific instances of atrocities were to be avoided, with emphasis placed on "what happened, in general terms." The commission was charged jointly with "truth and reconciliation so that things are brought to light and both communities accept responsibility and apologize to the other community for the atrocities." Political leaders were urged "to accept political cost in order to relieve human suffering." Policies were encouraged that jointly honored and remembered "the missing and victims of atrocities." In order to avoid continuance of unrealistic hopes, the category of "missing, presumed dead" was to be ascribed to those cases where families were satisfied that individuals could not be traced.

Settlers

The issue of what to do about citizenship for those non-Cypriot individuals living in northern Cyprus was to be addressed in a humanitarian manner. Cypriot citizenship was recommended for settlers (Turkish immigrants) who had been married to Cypriots for over three years. However, individuals "born in Cyprus, of non-Cypriot origin, and their first degree relatives" would be permitted to remain on the island, but "given the option to accept a repatriation scheme to be developed." The new federal government would be responsible for granting citizenship.

Refugees and Property

It was recommended that refugees have the right of return to their property and/or the right to be compensated for loss of property. In order to facilitate a large return of

Greek Cypriot refugees, territorial adjustments "along the lines of the percentages outlined in the Ghali Ideas" were recommended. Subject to the security needs of each community, all Cypriots would be given the gradual right to return to their former homes taking into consideration the present occupants of the property and the time necessary to build bi-communal confidence and relations. Property-owning refugees choosing not to return would be compensated. The Ghali proposals on compensation were adopted. Once all the territorial adjustments had been completed, it was contemplated that the federal government would establish regulations concerning purchase and ownership of property so that all Cypriots would have the right to purchase property anywhere on the island.

Freedom of Movement

Balanced against the security needs of each community, complete freedom of movement (for individuals, goods, and services) was the goal to be achieved "as quickly as possible." Foreign workers could be employed only if "local people" were unavailable. Extremism from either side was to be discouraged through joint policing, with violators being "identified, exposed and severely punished."

Identity

Notwithstanding the historical weakening of the Cypriot identity, "a unique Cypriot identity" was claimed that should be the basis for mutual acceptance and respect. The Cypriot multicultural society was referred to in the hope that "humanistic values" rather than "national values" would be developed. The positive history of how the two communities had lived together was to be preferred over the negative "two versions of history" that prevailed. Creation of cultural endeavors was encouraged in an effort to promote the unique Cypriot culture domestically and internationally. This "very difficult and sensitive aspect" of the Cyprus Problem was to be dealt with through confidence-building measures using "international norms and criteria." Certain provisions of the Economic Issues paper were adopted concerning compensation for property.

Social Issues[61]

This paper dealt with education, language, environment, health services, public relations, cultural heritage, and reconstitution of the society.

Education

Education was referred to as something that could assist in bi-communal tolerance and the ability of each community to live peacefully with the other. The educational system of each community was charged with having been "at the root" of the Cyprus Problem because for decades it poisoned "the relations of the two communities," created "negative stereotypes," built "hatred for the 'other' as the 'enemy'," and encouraged "nationalism and chauvinism." An entirely new bi-communal approach was called for that would feature Cyprus (rather than either Greece or Turkey) as the "mother country" respecting all cultures and communities.

Language

Language was singled out as being responsible for the barrier between the two communities because of the two mother tongues. As a result, English was designated as the language that should be used to remove the barrier. Greek and Turkish would become the compulsory second languages in the opposite communities, respectively, taught from the third grade.

---

[61] Approved: 28; abstained: 1; absent: 2.

69

Environment

Adoption of a bi-communal program "based on the 24 principles of the UN charter for the environment" was proposed, "the aim of which shall be the sustainable development of the country."

Health Services

Basing the recommendation on past use by Turkish Cypriots of the apparently superior health care facilities of the Greek Cypriots, a proposal was made for a more organized arrangement that could assist in reuniting the two communities in a bid for peace. This would include one general hospital and several specialized clinics for the island as a whole. Common agendas were encouraged for the various health-related NGOs in the two communities.

Public Relations

This area was singled out as a necessary prerequisite to a successful peace process. Specific areas designated for concentration of efforts by the bi-communal groups were: (1) the need for rapprochement, (2) the purpose of bi-communal meetings and the organizations participating in such gatherings, (3) the promotion of each other's community within the opposite community, (4) organization of conflict resolution institutions that "will use the methodology to seek mutually accepted solutions to conflicts," (5) creation of common-interest clubs, and (6) emphasis on the major role of women in the peace process as the more successful of the genders in this endeavor. In the list of various methods to be employed in the public relations campaign for peace, a provision for creation of a "remembrance and forgiveness group" was inserted "to establish and acknowledge our past mistakes and cultivate the belief in forgiveness to enable us to move on."

Cultural Heritage

It was declared that "our common future on this island must be based on the respect for the heritage of both communities." Cultural heritage was to be a uniting rather than a divisive force, and something to be promoted to the outside world. Collecting stories from past generations of the island "who had lived together in peace and harmony" prior to the outbreak of hostilities resulting in the current division was encouraged. Tolerance for both cultures and heritages was suggested. Publicizing and preserving historical sites was urged, as was the early education of students to appreciate the diverse heritage of the island. A dictionary of common words of each community used by the other was also proposed.

Reconstruction of the Society

It was noted that since 1955, "Cypriot society was an essentially divided society" because of religion and language as well as social disparities in the areas of business, police and civil service. Religion was targeted as a "major obstacle" because of the 1960 Constitution of the Republic of Cyprus prohibition against intermarriage. Acknowledgement was made that the 1974 war was the cause of non-communication between the two communities, "poisoned through the mass media on both sides." Noting that, regardless of the particular form of the final solution to the Cyprus Problem, "a reconstitution of the society along with some kind of integration" would be an indispensable condition to preserve the distinct existence of Cyprus. In order to achieve this, the elimination of negative references to Greek or Turkish Cypriots was recommended in an effort to prevent the two communities living apart and behaving as strangers on the small island. In order to accomplish reconstruction of the society, the following recommendations were made: (1) seek "proper behavior of the mass media," (2) change in the system of

71

education, (3) establishment of permanent bi-communal youth camps, (4) encourage efforts to change attitudes to appreciate how much both communities share in common, (5) emphasize the Cypriot nature of the two communities rather than looking to Greece or Turkey, and (6) discover methods to create "common myths."

Security[62]

The Security paper dealt with five areas: Guarantees, Demilitarization, Extremists, Trust, and Territory.

Guarantees

A treaty of guarantee would secure the security of the new Federal Republic and of the two sovereign states created. Until the Federal Republic should be admitted as a full EU member, the guarantor countries of Greece, Turkey, and the UK, plus the UN Security Council, would be looked to for security. When full EU membership is attained, the security arrangements of the EU are to be added. The independence and territorial integrity of the Federal Republic and the two separate states would be guaranteed, and any union with another country or any form of partition or secession was prohibited. Neither state could unilaterally amend the constitution of the Federal Republic, nor could either subsequently withdraw from the treaty of guarantee when it was decided that a system of guarantee was no longer needed. A Supervision and Verification Committee was to be formed for purposes of responding to security threats to the Federal Republic or either single state. Members of the committee would be representatives of the guarantor powers and of the president and vice-president of the new Federal Republic. UN support personnel would assist the committee in carrying

---

[62] Approved: 22; abstained: 8; absent: 1. One Turkish Cypriot "objected to the provision concerning guarantees."

72

out its responsibilities to investigate "any development, which in the view of any of its member [*sic*] is a threat to the security of either side or of the Federal Republic." Investigation would be conducted "through inspection or any other method deemed necessary." Prompt implementation of recommendations of the committee for rectification of treaty violations would be required. Support to the committee would come from UN Security Council revision of the UNFICYP mandate.

Demilitarization

The Federal Republic and each of the separate states would form separate police forces. All paramilitary activities and possession of weapons (other than those for which hunting licenses have been issued) would be outlawed by the Federal Republic. Violation would be a federal offense. Importation or transit of weapons, absent federal government approval, would be prohibited. A specific time frame for complete demilitarization would be agreed upon. Civilian groups would be prohibited from engaging in reserve force, military, or paramilitary training. Each side would implement the agreement for demilitarization simultaneously. In the event that complete demilitarization was not accomplished, both sides would have the right to return to the last stage fulfilled. Gradual disarmament on the "Green Line" was contemplated through a process that provided for mixed patrols consisting of police from both sides in conjunction with UN personnel. This would be an "intermediate area" constantly expanding, with free movement of people, merchandise, and settlement, so that eventual workplaces would be created.

Extremists

Police forces on both sides were encouraged to control their extremists pursuant to contemplated Federal Republic law. With the publicity assistance of the mass media, a committee consisting of educators from both sides would revise the textbooks containing the history of Cyprus in an effort to prevent the growth of extremist ideas. Existing foreign extremist elements would be banished from Cyprus and those not yet present would be prohibited from entering.

Trust

Trust is something that should be promoted by the Federal Republic on an international basis, and schoolbooks should refer to each community in a proper manner. Companies in one community should be encouraged to hire members of the other community. The mass media should be encouraged to participate in the process of confidence-building, and there should be a day recognizing the victims of bi-communal violence.

Territory

The Federal Republic consisting of the two federated states would have an "indivisible personality." While not affecting the demographic character of the respective federated states, Cypriots would have the freedom to live in either zone of the bi-zonal, bi-communal Federal Republic. The federal government would have the responsibility for territorial arrangements resulting from the freedom of settlement, travel and possession guaranteed by the federal constitution. Because of past historical failures to solve the Cyprus Problem, it was recommended that international organizations in addition to Turkey and Greece should be part of the guarantor process. Success would depend on both sides trusting each other to work together and believing in what they have agreed to do.

Economic Issues[63]

The economic matters dealt with in this part of the report were: compensation, European Union (EU), embargoes, and currency. The term "embargo" was used only in the context of the non-recognition problems suffered by the Turkish Cypriots as a result of the events that have occurred since the 1974 war. The issue of compensation was relevant only in connection with those who would seek redress. In that event, the Gali [Ghali] Set of Ideas was to be the basis for discussion. The Federal Republic of Cyprus should be the entity that would become a full member of the EU, with the Turkish Cypriot community having full representation and participating equally in accession negotiations. Because it would be in the interest of the Federal Republic, the accession of Turkey to the EU was supported. So long as there would be no prejudice to either side, interim measures that promote confidence and good will were supported. A single federal currency issued through a single central bank, autonomous of the EU and the euro, was encouraged. Compensation would be provided for loss of bank deposits, and Turkish Cypriot banks were to be compensated for their statutory reserves deposited with the Central Bank of Cyprus prior to 1974.

Compensation

The property claims of displaced persons from both communities were recognized and should "be dealt with fairly on the basis of a time-frame and practical regulations based on the 1977 high-level agreement on the need to ensure social peace and harmony," and on the provisions of

---

[63] Approved: 29; Disapproved: 2. One Turkish Cypriot "objected to the provisions concerning the European Union, and territorial adjustment and compensation." A second Turkish Cypriot "objected to the provisions concerning accession negotiation and accession to the European Union."

the paper.[64] The question of compensation would be considered only in those cases where individuals freely chose that option. As a first priority, the Greek Cypriot administration would have the responsibility for relocation and support concerning Turkish Cypriots residing in the area under Greek Cypriot control as well as displaced persons who would be returning. Turkish Cypriot 1974 residents would be able to elect to remain in the area under Greek Cypriot administration or request comparable property in the area coming under Turkish Cypriot administration. Displaced Turkish Cypriots residing under Greek Cypriot administration would have the option of receiving a comparable residence in that area, returning to their former property, or receiving a comparable residence in the area under Turkish Cypriot administration. Establishment of a bi-communal committee to "arrange for suitable housing for all persons affected by the territorial adjustments" would take place immediately after referenda approval.

In the areas under either Greek Cypriot or Turkish Cypriot administration, each community would be responsible for establishing an agency to handle issues

---

[64] *See generally* PALLEY, *supra* note 39, at 344. On February 12, 1977, Makarios and Denktash, in the presence of UN Secretary-General Dr. Kurt Waldheim, at UNFICYP Headquarters, Nicosia, Cyprus, agreed to seek "an independent, non-aligned, bi-communal Federal Republic" with "territory under the administration of each community [to be] discussed in the light of economic viability or productivity and land-ownership." Issues such as "freedom of movement, freedom of settlement, the right of property and other specific matters [remained] open for discussion taking into consideration the fundamental basis of a bi-communal federal system and certain practical difficulties which may arise for the Turkish Cypriot community." With respect to the "powers and functions of the central federal government," they were "to safeguard the unity of the country having regard to the bi-communal character of the State."

related to displaced persons. Where displaced persons elect to seek compensation for lost property, ownership of that property would be transferred to the community having administration of that area. Title to such properties would be exchanged "between the two [community] agencies at the 1974 values plus inflation." Compensation to displaced persons would be made by the agency in their community from sales or exchange of transferred property effected by the agency. The owners of property would have the election to be compensated at either 1974 figures plus inflation or at current prices. In the event of a shortfall of funds necessary for property compensation, the federal government would provide the deficit from a compensation fund of revenue sources "such as windfall taxes on the increased value of transferred properties following the overall agreement, and savings from defense spending." Added revenue to cover the shortfall would come from the solicitation of contributions to the compensation fund from other governments and international organizations. Long-term leasing and other commercial arrangements could also be considered as a source of shortfall funding. Authorized claimants for compensation were to be: (1) Greek Cypriots and Turkish Cypriots (or their heirs) who resided and/or owned property in 1974 that would now be located in the area administered by the other community, and (2) post-December 1963 displaced persons (or their heirs) from either community.

The option to return could also be elected by those current permanent residents of Cyprus in the federated state now administered by the other community who were owners of that property at the time of their displacement. If current permanent residents had been renters at the time of displacement, and they wished to resume permanent residency in the area, they would receive priority under arrangements for freedom of settlement. Filing periods for claims, a limitation on the number of annual applications, and a deadline year for return to permanent residence were discussed.[65] Provisions were also made for a joint federated state review for evaluation of the situation at the end of a prescribed period. That period would begin upon essential completion of the resettlement and rehabilitation process resulting from territorial adjustment. Settlement of those electing to return would not occur until satisfactory relocation of those affected by such election. Notwithstanding the need to preserve original ownership rights, special provisions were designed to cover the following situations: (1) where current occupant displaced persons express a wish to remain, (2) where substantial alterations or improvements to the property have been made by the current occupant, (3) where the property has been converted to public use, or (4) where persons who have been involved in hate crimes against persons in the community of return have, after due process of law, been prevented from returning by that federated state.

European Union

It was made clear that EU membership for the new Federal Republic "should not be dependent on the membership of any other country." While the EU could make a significant contribution, irrespective of accession to membership the priority for the new Federal Republic should be equalization between the communities of their economic standards. As the EU membership accession process continues, the Turkish Cypriot community should

---

[65] Apparently, no limitation was placed on the right of return for those Maronites who in 1974 lost their permanent residence in the area of the federated state that would be under the future administration of the Turkish Cypriot community. Maronites are "a Christian sect that had emigrated to Cyprus, predominantly from Lebanon" during the Ottoman period (1571-1878). *See* INSIGHT GUIDES: CYPRUS 65 (Hansjorg Brey & Claudia Muller eds., 1993) (explaining that Maronites historically had been living in enclaves in northern Cyprus).

be permitted to participate in the negotiations without prejudice to its position in relation to settlement of the Cyprus Problem.

Embargoes

Without prejudicing the position of either community in relation to the settlement of the Cyprus Problem, interim measures should be created to: (1) establish "free business or shopping areas" for both communities in places such as Pyla Village, (2) facilitate the free movement of tourists between the two communities, (3) lift all local and international restrictions concerning communication and transportation (e.g., postal and telephone), (4) permit freedom of travel for Turkish Cypriots on the same basis as Greek Cypriots, (5) allow channeling of international financial aid and support to both communities, and (6) make possible the participation of Turkish Cypriots in international cultural and sporting events.

Fiscal Issues

The federal and state constitutions should provide for the levy of taxes on all levels of the federal system (central government, each federated state, and local authorities).

Public Reaction

Subsequent to its completion, the members of the Oslo Group attempted to get a hearing for their report from government officials, press, and others on both sides, who they thought would be interested in the results. They were mostly ignored for three years. Then, in the early part of 2002, a Greek Cypriot Sunday front-page newspaper story referred to what the Oslo Group did as "shocking," criticizing the participants in the group as being "handpicked by the Americans…betraying the pain" caused by Turkey's invasion of the island, and describing their work as a "pointless psychological effort" to deal with a "geopolitical problem," all as the result of "American input...[seeking to] promote unacceptable compromises...[through the] US Embassy in Nicosia and the American Fulbright Commission...[as the] major sponsors of conflict resolution groups...[spending $15 million annually to] help solve the Cyprus problem."[66] It appeared not to be coincidental that Greek Cypriot President Glafcos Clerides and Turkish Cypriot leader Rauf Denktash were engaged in peace negotiations under the approaching cloud of the 2003 Greek Cypriot presidential election.

The Turkish Cypriot press also expressed itself around the same time. Under a banner headline the newspaper Yeni Duzen announced that e-mail threats were made against the lives of Turkish Cypriot Oslo Group members and their families as a result of the Oslo Report.[67] Following this, on February 14, 2002, five of the original Greek Cypriot members of the Oslo Group held a press conference in Nicosia where they defended the activities of the group and its report against critics who had labeled it as "treacherous." Although it was acknowledged that this had been "the first time that 25 people from both sides came together and agreed on the contents of a document," the press within the last week before the conference had "dredged up the report branding much of its content unacceptable." The five Greek Cypriots "accused the media of being hypocritical and of having totally ignored the

---

[66] *See* Jennie Matthew, *Conflict Resolution Critics 'Playing a Political Game,'* CYPRUS MAIL: NEWS ARTICLES IN ENGLISH, Jan. 29, 2002, http://www.hri.org/news/cyprus/cmnews/2002/02-01-29.cmnews.html.

[67] *See Threatening E-mails to the Turkish Cypriot Members of the Oslo Group*, CYPRUS PRESS AND INFORMATION OFFICE: TURKISH CYPRIOT PRESS REVIEW DIRECTORY, Feb. 11, 2002, http://www.hri.org/news/cyprus/tcpr/2002/02-02-11.tcpr.html.

report" because only two newspapers "published anything" three years earlier. They also noted that both Clerides and Denktash had "refused to look at it" even though they had been "offered copies from their respective sides." The group suspected that the "resurrection" of the report was "linked to someone's political agenda in view of the resumption of direct talks, which began on January 16," 2002. The five Greek Cypriots also made it clear that they had acted in their personal capacities and had not claimed that their work "would result in a political solution." They praised the Turkish Cypriot members of the Oslo Group "who were brave enough to defend and support within their community the methodology used by the group and its final outcome, as well as the right of every Cypriot to meet and express themselves freely despite the pressure and threats they faced."[68]

Post-Oslo Workshops

During the summer of 2000, pursuant to an arrangement funded by the United Nations Office of Project Services (UNOPS), I returned to Cyprus to provide an advanced program to a selected number of those who had been trained by me earlier. I planned to expand on the humanistic aspects of the Umbreit model. However, just prior to my departure for Cyprus, a new model of conflict resolution was published. This is referred to as "narrative mediation" and was designed to succeed where the more traditional problem-solving and interest-based models failed, especially in the area of violence and international hostilities.[69] I decided to use this new model as the basis for

---

[68] *See* Jean Christou, *Oslo Group Slams its Critics,* CYPRUS MAIL: NEWS ARTICLES IN ENGLISH, Feb. 15, 2002, *available at* http://www.hri.org/news/cyprus/cmnews/2002/0202-15.cmnews.html.

[69] *See generally* JOHN WINSLADE & GERALD MONK, NARRATIVE MEDIATION: A NEW APPROACH TO CONFLICT RESOLUTION (2000).

the advanced bi-communal training. My interest in teaching this radical new model was motivated by the fact that it developed the individual stories of the parties to a conflict as a means of creating a lasting resolution. Its goal is to create a relationship incompatible with conflict, which is accomplished through a transformed relationship constructed from stories that demonstrate understanding, respect, and collaboration. The complex nature of conflicts is deconstructed and replaced by new possibilities for change through (1) achieving a trusting relationship with the parties, (2) mapping the effects of a particular conflict's history, (3) constructing a new narrative for solution, and (4) seeking consensus and resolution. My prior work (1997-1999) with the general population was centered on teaching the bi-communal participants how to connect and communicate, getting them to role-play scenarios from their respective cultures, and demonstrating how the various mediation models could successfully resolve conflict in the situations that they developed. While they were able to work and negotiate successfully with each other in a bi-communal setting, they always did so without allowing those from the other side to really experience their very personal deep-seated feelings related by historical divisive images.

When I explained the narrative model in September of 2000, the participants in the bi-communal workshop were at best resistant and proceeded reluctantly. However, in the process of telling their stories they became empowered to express themselves without reservation, managed to give each other's point of view recognition, and genuinely attempted to understand how the other side felt historically. The conclusion of the lengthy workshop disclosed unanimity of feeling that, contrary to their original reluctance, participants accomplished something special for the first time in the twenty-six years of the island's divisive history. They were able to speak openly about their respective traumas and understand the diverse points of view generated by the historical passage from one generation to another. It was clearly possible that unresolved resentments previously festering in this civil society could now be controlled.

I returned to Cyprus in June 2003 to once again work with selected participants from my prior programs.[70] Two consecutive one-week bi-communal workshops had been scheduled with duplicate agendas in order to keep the size of each manageable and to accommodate the schedules of the various participants. However, most of the people designated for the first workshop preferred the second, resulting in a much smaller first workshop and a much larger second one. It is the second workshop that produced the activity referred to in this discussion. While the first workshop (seven days) was effective, the extent of the debate was limited due to its small size (seven Greek Cypriots and three Turkish Cypriots, which varied from day-to-day). Some of the participants from the first workshop decided to also attend the second one because they wanted to interact with the larger group. The second workshop, which lasted six days, was attended by fifteen Greek Cypriots and sixteen Turkish Cypriots, which also varied from day-to-day.

The purpose of the two 2003 bi-communal workshops was to provide an opportunity for the participants to become familiar with and discuss in detail the proposed Annan Plan for reunification of Cyprus.[71] The ground rules were set forth at the beginning of each workshop.[72] The participants in the larger second workshop decided that they did not want to debate the Annan Plan per se, but rather desired to brainstorm their

---

[70] Pursuant to a Sally Casanova Memorial Grant from California State University, Dominguez Hills.

[71] *See* Appendix B.

[72] *See* Appendix C.

83

own list of peace plan issues for their agenda. Honoring their wish, that approach was taken. The participants created a possible list of 48 issues for group consideration. From this list ten main issues with their respective sub-issues were selected for discussion and voting. Because of the length and intensity of the subsequent discussion process, only five of the ten issues selected (with their various sub-issues) were discussed and tabulated pursuant to a vote.[73]

When I subsequently presented the 2003 positive outcome during an international workshop at Oxford University the following October,[74] I was astounded to discover that several of the other participants felt that diplomacy is best left to the elites. The fact that Alvaro de Soto, the UN Secretary-General's representative and the de facto author of the Annan Plan,[75] was also in attendance made the lack of faith in civil society all the more surprising. The 2003 workshops questioned whether each community could put aside its history in order to achieve the goodwill necessary for a positive outcome in meeting the May 1, 2004 deadline established by the EU for accession to membership of a reunited Cyprus. A negative answer would admit only the Greek Cypriots. In such event, the division between the two communities would be further exacerbated, and it could be only a matter of time before Turkey would seek to partition and annex the northern part of Cyprus because of its determination to maintain control over the entire island as essential to her security. This appears to be notwithstanding any necessity

---

[73] *See* Appendix D.

[74] *See* Othon Anastasakis et al., Getting to Yes: Suggestions for Embellishment of the Annan Plan for Cyprus (2004), *available at* http://www.sant.ox.ac.uk/esc/esclectures/Oxford_Cyprus.pdf.

[75] *See* PALLEY, *supra* note 39, at 18-19.

84

to protect Turkish Cypriots.[76]

Unfortunately, the division appears to have been further breached by the failure of the referenda process on April 24, 2004,[77] and the official admittance of only the Republic of Cyprus (Greek Cypriots) to the EU on May 1, 2004.[78] Based on my information from the executive director of the Cyprus Fulbright Commission, my 2003 workshops were the first to provide any kind of bi-communal dialogue concerning the details of the Annan Plan. Incredibly, in view of the critical nature of the Plan as the last hope for peace on Cyprus for the foreseeable future, numerous bi-communal members with whom I interacted confirmed that my workshops were the first. Many have wondered whether a concentrated effort on a larger scale to thoroughly educate the Greek Cypriot electorate concerning the Plan may have changed the outcome. My work on the much smaller front indicates that perhaps that could have been the case.

Track III Approach and Analogous Situations

John Braithwaite argues that to be effective today, diplomacy must encompass the reparative practice of restorative justice rather than the traditional retributive approach that emphasizes anger and hatred engendered by past war crimes. Otherwise, he feels peace will not be possible because of the need for rituals to heal damaged souls, to discover the ability to transform hatred into sorrow or forgiveness, and exorcise the evil of the past while moving forward with hope.[79] Following Braithwaite's arguments, forgiveness is something that requires survivors

---

[76] *Ibid.* at 236.

[77] *Ibid.* at 217. Percentage of valid votes cast: Turkish Cypriots 64.91 "Yes;" Greek Cypriots 75.83 "No."

[78] *See* HANNAY, *supra* note 35, at 241

[79] JOHN BRAITHWAITE, RESTORATIVE JUSTICE AND RESPONSIVE REGULATION 172, 207 (2002).

be emotionally ready because it cannot be forced, so in advocating a reconfiguration, "bottom up restorative justice" can heal ethnic division in those instances where "restorative peacemaking" can be connected to "top-down preventive diplomacy and negotiated cessation of hostilities," as an antidote to the official "elite diplomacy," where deals are made among representatives of governments without considering reactions of the general population.[80] Elite diplomacy has failed to sustain the successes of international mediation and preventive diplomacy says Braithwaite, so he contends that, "to be effective, diplomacy must adopt practices and values more akin to those of restorative justice," which he refers to as "democratized restorative justice."[81]

The practices and values I used for my work in Cyprus can be described as part of a democratized restorative justice approach. They are designed to transform the conflicted relationships, to manage and ultimately resolve the controversy, while addressing the disputed issues. Members of civil society[82] need to learn the skills and techniques of how to connect with each other in order to effectively communicate as part of a *two-way street* where traffic moves collaboratively in both directions, concurrently. These are the tools that will make the process work. Participants need to become empowered to tell each other their stories, *i.e.* their personal points of view, in a respectful listening atmosphere. This creates an

---

[80] *Ibid.*

[81] *Ibid.*

[82] *See* HAROLD H. SAUNDERS, A PUBLIC PEACE PROCESS: SUSTAINED DIALOGUE TO TRANSFORM RACIAL AND ETHNIC CONFLICTS 12 (1999). It is "the public area in which citizens outside government do their work." This is "the arena in which the associations [sic] citizens form and many less formal nongovernmental organizations work."

understanding of the storyteller's point of view and establishes their humanity. In order to accomplish this, the participants must first acknowledge that the "other side" is not the enemy, but rather the *problem itself* is the enemy causing the conflict.

Next, it is important to work with the participants on the reversal of their roles and their ability to "step into each other's shoes" to fully appreciate their respective interests and underlying needs. This view assists in establishing a different perspective. It effectively says that there is no single "truth," but only the perception of the facts as seen through the eyes of the beholder. The result is the realization that there can be a respect for different points of view without agreeing with the "other side." This leads to a possible collaboration between opposing points of view to create a mutually acceptable version of the events from which the parties can move forward. In order to set the stage for the process of forgiveness and reconciliation, the participants need to practice tolerance, appreciate diversity and ethnicity, and understand that each feels hurt while accepting that each has caused pain. The participants also need to understand the damage caused by anger and hatred, and the benefits of love and kindness. Self-respect is the thread that binds all of this together, creating what I refer to as the *Seven Keys to Peacebuilding*:

- Empowerment to participate fully in the process.
- Recognition of each other's point of view.
- Trust established in order to "open the curtain" that hides the past.
- Truth disclosed without reservation in order to create understanding.
- Forgiveness given willingly while not being required to forget.
- Collaboration practiced to design productive solutions.

- Reconciliation achieved for future peaceful conduct.

Time for Second Oslo Group

The bi-communal participants in my September 2000 narrative mediation workshops were ordinary citizens who had the opportunity to disclose their sorrows and suffering directly to each other, followed by the expressions of apology and the granting of forgiveness. They effectively accomplished the goal of "humanizing" each other so that they understood and acknowledged their respective points of view. If citizens in areas of cultural, religious, ethnic, or political conflict are able to engage the larger community on each side with the healing aspects of mutual goal development and successful establishment of working relationships, members of civil society may yet provide a positive example of democratized restorative justice.

The lesson for peacebuilding seems clear. Rather than continuing to rely on the failed elite approach to diplomacy at the Track I (or even Track II) level, those negotiating such conflicts should consider all stakeholders and work from the ground up through civil society, rather than from the top down entangled in the special interests of those occupying the seats of government. The approach suggested here provides individuals at the grassroots with the opportunity to tell their stories about a particular injustice, its consequences, and what must be done to "make things right." The result can be more than simply a society with a greater voice from its citizens. It also offers a more efficient and just system of government as well as a truly positive step towards securing an improved peaceful world.

Based on my personal experiences with Cypriots from all levels of civil society at the grassroots on both sides of the "Green Line" or Buffer Zone,[83] I believe there is a viable argument for the emphasis on Track III diplomacy as the next step in the attempt to achieve a positive peaceful reunification of the island. The results from the Oslo Group indicate that Track III diplomacy from the bottom up could have possibly made a difference in achieving a positive outcome in the bi-communal referenda voting on April 24, 2004. This is because an impartial comparison of the written results of the Oslo Group with the fate of Annan I through V clearly supports the conclusion that, if left to work it out by themselves, the people at the bottom are far superior to those at the top. Is it any wonder that the Oslo Report ruffled the feathers of the political elite in both communities?

Notwithstanding the emphatic reiteration of then Greek Cypriot President, Tassos Papadopoulos, concerning his strong personal and public commitment to his community for a bi-zonal, bi-communal federal solution, the peace process was not resumed during his presidency.[84] This resulted in the status quo being solidified to the disadvantage of all Cypriots, causing the EU to begin considering ways to possibly end the isolation of the Turkish Cypriot community and urging each side to be willing to reach out to the other for a final resolution.[85] Although working with Turkish Cypriot authorities to enhance their economy, the EU has denied that the effect

---

[83] *See* HANNAY, *supra* note 35, at 6.

[84] *See* PALLEY, *supra* note 39, at 241.

[85] *See* Olli Rehn, Member, European Commission, Responsible for Enlargement, Speech at the Cyprus International Conference Center (May 13, 1995), *in* CYPRUS: ONE YEAR AFTER ACCESSION, at 3-5, *available at* http://europa.eu.int/comm/ commission_barroso/rehn/speeches/pdf/050513_nicosia.pdf.

would be recognition of the Turkish Cypriots as a separate state.[86]

While all Cypriots have been able to "mix together fully and cross to the opposite sides of the island," since April 2003, the fact of the matter is that Greek and Turkish Cypriots for the most part do not trust each other and engage only in minimal contact.[87] One Turkish Cypriot lawyer representing some of the families of those killed during the 1974 war and who are still missing indicated to me that she believes both sides should stop the political exploitation, saying: "If a Greek Cypriot dares to mention any of the suffering of Turkish Cypriots he will be accused of talking like a Turkish Cypriot extremist. And, the same goes for Turkish Cypriots...The Turkish Cypriot missing is an issue and a wound in the north for those people... [T]he Greek Cypriot missing is an issue, and a wound in the south...There is no sign of both groups getting together and realising [sic] that their grief is the same, the crime against them is the same. That's the culture that unfortunately still needs a lot of change." And a Greek Cypriot bi-communal activist has indicated: "There are no pages on [sic] our newspaper on the life of the other side. The Green Line is open physically for us to move but there is an invisible barrier that stops us." Both individuals were members of the Oslo Group and participants in my training workshops.

The international community has indicated it does not want the status quo. The prospect of relief for the Turkish Cypriots from the heavy burdens imposed by the embargo and lack of international recognition (other than

---

[86] *See EU Pledges AID for Turkish Cyprus*, BBC NEWS, *available at* http://newsnote.bbc.co.wk/mpapps/pagetools/print/news.bbc.co.uk/1/hi/world/europe/3660 (last visited Oct. 9, 2005).

[87] *See* Tabitha Morgan, *Cyprus Keeps its Hidden Barrier*, BBC NEWS (United Kingdom), *available at* http://news.bbc.co.uk/1/hi/world/europe/4313016.stm (last visited Oct. 7, 2005).

by Turkey) seems to indicate a movement towards partition. The question for Turkey is why only partition? Why would it not seek to annex the entire northern part of the island currently under joint Turkish and Turkish Cypriot control? In the face of this, it is "perplexing to see that the Greek Cypriot side does not wish to give in writing to the Secretary [G]eneral of the UN the changes it wants to have in [the] plan."[88]Both communities need to discover how to engage in dialogue together because a solution is in the best interest of each, and that is where the open issues should be addressed.[89] Turkey had suggested a May or June 2006 meeting, under UN auspices, on the Cyprus conflict to take place between representatives from the Turkish and Greek Cypriot communities, also to be attended by diplomats from Turkey and Greece, but UN reaction was to indicate that its resumption of peace efforts would have to wait until "after the May 2006 parliamentary elections in the Republic of Cyprus [in order to] avoid a hasty new process of negotiations, which would fail in no time."[90]Cyprus is still waiting.

---

[88] *See* Dr Ozdemir A. Ozgur, *Comment - The Cyprus Problem: Ideas, Realities and Might* 2, *available at* http://www.cyprus-mail.com/news/main.php?id=18989&cat_id=1 (last visited Sep. 1, 2005). "It must be pointed out that because of the Turkish Cypriots and proximity of Cyprus to Turkey, as well as because of strategic, historical, moral and psychological reasons, Turkey is not ready to forget and throw Cyprus out of her sight. The more so, because she is surrounded by Greece on her western frontiers and would not like to be surrounded by Greece in the south, too, through Cyprus, by hook or by crook. Frankly speaking, Turkey's feelings are to some extent shared by the big powers. Here comes again into the picture the role of might and mighty powers. The question is: can the Greek idea confront and beat the might of Turkey and others? We have to use our brains."

[89] *See* Rehn, *supra* note 85, at 4.

[90] *See UN to Revive Cyprus Talks in May,* EurActiv.com – EU News, Policy Positions & EU Actors online, *available at*

91

Turkey has indicated a willingness to open its sea and airports to Greek Cypriots in exchange for a reciprocal end to restrictions on Turkish Cypriots. However, even the EU, US and UN support of this effort was not sufficient to prevent rejection by Papadopoulos and other leaders who relegated the proposal to a rehashing of the past.[91] From his observation point, former Greek Cypriot foreign minister (1978-1983) Nicos Rolandis, who also has held other government positions, opined that, had the Annan Plan been accepted, thousands of Greek and Turkish Cypriots would have been able to return to their homes under administration by their own respective communities, and the stream of Turkish Cypriot construction on Greek Cypriot properties in the north could have been prevented. Ironically, the point of no return has passed for Greek Cypriots, while Turkish Cypriots have been able to convince Greek Cypriot courts to issue orders for return of property to its Turkish Cypriot owners.[92]

A handwritten quotation attributed to Margaret Mead, once again passed to me by a participant during the second June 2003 workshop discussion of the Annan Plan, seems particularly apropos here: "Never doubt that a small group of thoughtful, committed citizens can change the world. Indeed, it is the only thing that ever has."[93] Perhaps it is time for a second Track III Oslo Group.

---

http://www.euractiv.com/ Article?tcmuri=tcm:29-152089-16&type=News (last visited Feb. 8, 2006).

[91] *Ibid.*

[92] *See* Nicos A. Rolandis, *King Jigme and Floundering Cyprus*, *available at* http://www.cyprus-mail.com/news/main.php?id=24591&cat_id=1 (last visited Feb. 26, 2006).

[93] The participant was one of the teachers who had participated in the training for educators as part of the Cyprus Fulbright Commission's bi-

communal conflict resolution program (an intensive 40-hour workshop in teaching tolerance in the classroom through the use of people skills that improve human performance and communication) that I conducted at the School for Peace Neve Shalom - Wahat- Al-salam in Israel from August 25-30, 2000. The quotation had been located on the inside front cover of the program materials that I prepared and distributed to the participants at that workshop. Ironically, this had been borne out earlier during the summer of 1999, right before my wife and I were to return home to California. Greek Cypriot entrepreneur Constantine (Dinos) Lordos was experiencing difficulty recruiting Turkish Cypriots for his groundbreaking bi-communal confidence building efforts to facilitate the reconciliation process between the Greek and Turkish Cypriot communities through joint commercial endeavors. Because of my extensive work with Cypriots on both sides of the Green Line, Lordos felt that I would be able to attract Turkish as well as Greek Cypriot participation. So, he asked me to delay our departure and stay another month beyond the end of my Fulbright award, and recruit Cypriots from among the bi-communal groups with whom I had been engaged during the previous almost two years, concentrating on Turkish Cypriot participation. I agreed but cautioned that the people with whom I had been working were for the most part ordinary citizens from the grassroots. He assured me that they would be a welcome addition. The subsequent joint meeting of bi-communal representatives, at the restaurant located outside the small village of Pyla, attracted a large number of both Turkish and Greek Cypriots who had been contacted by me. It was clear they attended because this was their way of demonstrating that each was committed to contributing their personal efforts to effect change on the island.

93

II

RETHINKING CYPRUS PROBLEM[94]

Background of the Problem

More than nine years have passed since the bi-communal referenda voting on April 24, 2004. Notwithstanding the feeling of some in both communities that each subsequent passing year will be the one in which a solution to the Cyprus Problem will finally emerge, the impasse remains. Without significant change, the continued result will be this impasse, and not a resolution acceptable to both communities. Ironically, the proposed reunification of the divided island on a bi-communal and bi-zonal basis, supported for so long by Greek Cypriots, was in the end rejected by their negative referendum vote in April 2004. The reversal of historical roles between Greek Cypriots and Turkish Cypriots was complete when the normally secession-minded Turkish Cypriots voted for reunification. Efforts for a negotiated settlement appear to have disappeared. These have been replaced by unilateral attempts to keep alive the pro-solution enthusiasm of the Turkish Cypriots while trying to motivate Greek Cypriots to effect political change. Surrounding this seems to be a cadre of support for reconciliation between the two communities, encouraged by advocates for assertion of pressure upon political elites on both sides for immediate resumption of the negotiation process. This would help immeasurably to reduce the isolation experienced by Turkish Cypriots and in the long run promote a sustainable

---

[94] *See* A. Marco Turk. 2007. "Rethinking the Cyprus Problem: Are Frame-Breaking Changes Still Possible Through Application of Intractable Conflict Intervention Approaches to This 'Hurting Stalemate'?" LOY. L.A. INT'L & COMP. L. REV. 29:463-501.

solution based on equality.[95]

Reunification pursuant to the Annan Plan appears to be the only road to approval by both communities. Incredibly, the initial idea for a bi-zonal and bi-communal federation is attributed to the 1970s collaboration between Makarios and Denktash. Yet, subsequent blockage of a similar agreement appears to have been the work of the Greek Cypriot leadership spearheaded by Papadopoulos. But the Greek Cypriot resistance to engagement with the UN and with other international partners will almost certainly cause the island to embrace permanent partition and the formally or informally recognized independence of the north. Acceptance of minority status by Turkish Cypriots in a Greek Cypriot controlled state is not on the table. Clearly, the dynamics of the Cyprus conflict need to be changed if there is to be hope for success concerning any future UN-brokered solution that might be proposed. This would require a new environment that advances the best interests of all parties.[96]

Specific Issues

European Union

The EU must promote "the economic development and European integration of northern Cyprus as it pledged to do in April 2004."[97]

Greek Cypriots

In order to rise above the "uncompromising position taken by the present government," opposition forces, moderates from all political elements, and *leaders of civil*

---

[95] *See* Int'l Crisis Group, The Cyprus Stalemate: What Next?, Mar. 8, 2006, http://www.crisisgroup.org/home/index.cfm?id=4003&l=1.

[96] *Ibid.*

[97] *Ibid.*

society must generate debate of the critical "core issues." They must understand that regional stability will result from the two-state model and accept that the 1963 actions of the Greek Cypriots against Turkish Cypriots are as responsible for the conflict as the 1974 actions of Turkey against the Greek Cypriots. They must also acknowledge that upheaval from their homes and mourning their missing apply equally to Turkish Cypriots as well as Greek Cypriots, and reconsider the advantages of implementing the bi-zonal and bi-communal principles to which Greek Cypriots agreed more than thirty-three years ago.[98]

Greece

The Greek government needs to actively affirm to the international community its support of the Annan Plan to restart negotiations and seek a solution satisfactory to both sides. In addition, Greece should assume the lead role in seeing that the EU renews efforts to discharge its obligations to Turkish Cypriot citizens.[99]

Turkish Cypriots

Turkish Cypriots must deal with the numerous unresolved property cases, bring their laws and practices into compliance with the *acquis communautaire* of the EU, see to it that the EU-Turkey Customs Union is extended to the north, and obtain agreement from Turkey to reduce (a) its number of military forces on the island and (b) its population of mainland settlers resulting from a thirty-year migration to the northern part of the island. They should also demonstrate more understanding of Greek Cypriot demands concerning their missing and the need for restoration of cultural monuments damaged over the years

---

[98] *Ibid.*

[99] *Ibid.*

since 1974.[100]

Turkey

Unilateral confidence-building efforts need to be undertaken to demonstrate its support of a satisfactory settlement. Full implementation of the twenty-five member-state Customs Union and Turkey's other existing EU commitments should be pursued. There should be partial reduction of the 35,000 troops that are stationed in the north to a number that would not threaten the security interest of Turkey, and a plan for repatriation of a specified number of mainland Turkish settlers based on a formal census should be pursued.[101]

United States

The US can facilitate efforts to restart settlement negotiations for reunification of Cyprus within the broad framework of the Annan Plan by upgrading its diplomatic presence on the northern part of the island, and (b) increasing its contacts at every level with Turkish Cypriot officials and *civil society*.[102]

United Nations

This world organization must call for an end to the "isolation of northern Cyprus" and encourage the Greek Cypriots to "indicate their concerns with the Annan Plan in a form which offers some hope for a negotiated settlement." At the same time, the UN must create a United Nations Development Programme Trust Fund for the north.[103]

---

[100] *Ibid.*

[101] *Ibid.*

[102] *Ibid.*

[103] *Ibid..*

Current Reunification Dilemmas

Nicos A. Rolandis[104] has been the standard bearer for those Greek Cypriots who support reunification. He writes regularly on the subject and constantly reminds his fellow citizens that their country "is continuously going down a slippery slope."[105] In arguing that "the situation on the ground has deteriorated," Rolandis conducted a review of the "political due diligence of the past 32 months."[106] He concluded that the Greek Cypriots, by their actions have:[107]

- "Solidified the concept of partition."
- Lost the beautiful seaport city of Famagusta (to which "her residents would have returned two and a half years ago" if the plan had been accepted).
- Lost the historically important village of Morphou.
- Missed the opportunity to have 90,000 refugees returned to "fifty-odd villages" representing "9% of the territory which would have been returned" to Greek Cypriots in the settlement.
- Lost the opportunity to achieve "termination of the Turkish occupation through the withdrawal of more than 39,000 troops, return of the refugees, restoration of human

---

[104] Republic of Cyprus Minister of Foreign Affairs (1978-1983), Minister of Commerce, Industry & Tourism (1998-2003), member of House of Representatives (1991-1996), President of the Liberal Party (1986-1998), and Vice-president of Liberal International.

[105] Nicos A. Rolandis, Cyprus: Political Due Diligence 2004-2006; The Gods and Friedrich Schiller 1 (Dec. 28, 2006) (on file with author) [hereinafter Rolandis, Political Due Diligence 2004-2006].

[106] *Ibid.*

[107] *Ibid.*

rights."[108]

- Contributed to diminished confidence between the two communities.
- Been "inundated with a large number of additional Turkish settlers" who may not leave.
- Permitted construction of new buildings in the "occupied areas" (mainly for foreign buyers) worth "hundreds of millions of pounds."
- Allowed "an explosion of tourist development in the north, which continues incessantly," and that will not "come back to us."
- Enabled "the EU through its European Court of Human Rights . . . indirect recognition of the Turkish Cypriot "state."
- Permitted establishment of a "contact group between the European Parliament and the Turkish Cypriot 'state.'"
- Facilitated acceptance of "members of the Turkish Cypriot 'Parliament' as observers in the Parliamentary Assembly of the Council of Europe."
- Created a situation where for "the first time since 1960 . . . the Cypriot President has not been invited for a meeting with the leadership of the U.S."; but the Turkish Cypriot leader was included in a meeting with the U.S. secretary of state "in Brussels, in London, in Pakistan and elsewhere."
- Created a situation where for "the first time

---

[108] *Ibid.* (quoting an evaluation made in April 2004 by AKEL, the "big party of the governing coalition").

in history" the Secretary-General and other high officials of the U.N. "are negative or even hostile vis-à-vis [the government of the Republic of Cyprus]."

- Created a situation where the "55-odd countries" of the Islamic Conference have "for the first time upgraded the Turkish Cypriots to the status of 'Turkish Cypriot state.'"
- Created a situation where the European Commission "is not friendly at all towards" the Republic of Cyprus.
- Enabled Turkey's commendation in 2004 by the European Council (which includes the Republic of Cyprus) for "her constructive stance on Cyprus."
- Allowed "the operation of the Tymbou (Ercan) Airport" to be "considered as lawful for Cypriot, European and other foreign passengers" since 2004.
- Created a scenario where "partition is in the wings" as "direct trade."
- Created a situation where the Republic of Cyprus "went through the humiliation of December 2006 in Brussels" when the republic demonstrated that it did not "possess even some vestiges of knowhow, experience and realism."[109]

---

[109] *Ibid.* Presumably, a reference to "Ankara (Turkey) accuses Nicosia (Cyprus) of using its membership to snag Turkey's accession bid and extract concessions in the Cyprus dispute. Cyprus, which like all EU members wields veto powers, swiftly rejected Turkey's new initiative as a 'mockery'." *See E.U. Wrangles over Turkish Initiative,* FRANCE 24, Dec. 8, 2006, http://www.france24.com/france24Public/en/news/Europe/20061206-Cyprus-Reax.html.

- Created a situation where "for the first time, the Cyprus problem is completely stagnant, nothing moves, whilst partition is gradually but steadily setting in."[110]

According to Rolandis, this is notwithstanding that he and others "have been speaking the bitter truth for 30 years and abandoned positions and high offices."[111] He asks the hard questions concerning whether there has been a "change [in] the mentality of this people who live with one hand lying on their wallet and the other hand on 'power' and 'favoritism', instead of placing one hand on their heart and the other on their country?"[112]Rolandis also considered what would happen when the Greek Cypriot presidential election took place in 2008. He had a number of suggestions for the new president:[113]

- Serve only a brief term concentrating on the resolution of the Cyprus Problem, with the knowledge that this "will entail difficult and probably tragic moments for himself."
- Understand that he "will have to give the correct guidelines to the people, so that the blunders of the past will not be repeated," knowing that "many political parties will not be helpful in his quest for a solution."
- Be "prudent and moderate," because "[n]ationalists and fanatics cannot address bicommunal [sic] or multicommunal [sic] issues" since "[t]hey lead to confrontation."
- Accept that he "must be fair and objective" in

---

[110] Rolandis, Political Due Diligence 2004-2006, *supra* note 105, at 4.

[111] *Ibid.*

[112] *Ibid.*

[113] *See* Nicos A. Rolandis, Greek Hero Kolokotronis, The Gunshot and the New President 2-5 (Jan. 18, 2007) (on file with author).

recognizing that both Greek Cypriots and Turkish Cypriots are "debited with sins," and "he must be prepared to pay the price for these sins of ours."

- "[K]now that a bicommunal [sic], bizonal [sic] federation for which we have signed both in the red ink of Makarios and in the blue ink of other Presidents, entails a number of substantive rights for the Turkish Cypriot community, which should not and cannot be overlooked."
- "[U]pgrade radically our relations with Europe, where we are today conceived as the black sheep of the family."
- Reopen the "gates" of Washington, D.C., that have been "firmly closed for the President of the Republic of Cyprus for the past four years," and also "gain better access to the family of the United Nations." This will require acknowledgement that "sovereignty and state entity do not permanently belong to [the Republic of Cyprus]" because they are subject to the recognition of "the other 191 states of the world."
- "[K]eep the balances which are a prerequisite for the survival of our country" by realizing, in part, that "Cyprus does not appear on many world maps, not even as a small speck."
- "[E]xtend a hand of friendship to the Turkish Cypriots and to their leaders, even if such leaders will have to reach an understanding with Ankara [Turkey] in connection with the solution of our problem." Otherwise, if "each side insists on its own positions to the bitter end, if we continue pulling Cyprus until we tear it apart, we shall eventually cry over a lost

country."

The former Turkish Cypriot leader Rauf Denktash has been quoted as saying, "[w]hat is hurting is the interpretation put on our 'yes vote' by the Americans and others to the effect that the Turkish Cypriot side has thus abandoned its sovereignty and separate independence, which is not true." He feels that although the EU seems interested in lifting the embargo against Turkish Cypriots, the end result may not be certain if "the EU regards North Cyprus as an occupied part of the Republic of Cyprus. As long as they do not treat the North Cyprus on its own merits, all such moves are done with the consent of and subject to the conditions of the so-called government of Cyprus." Notwithstanding close monitoring of the Cyprus situation by the EU, Denktash is of the opinion that "it would be catastrophic" for Turkey to withdraw its troops from the island, feeling that such action would cause Turkish Cypriots to have a "loss of faith in Turkey, in the EU and in themselves. New bloodshed would be followed by the Turkish Cypriots fleeing from the island."[114]

There appeared to be some movement toward a *two-state* solution for Cyprus, at least from Turkish Cypriots, as indicated in a 2007 poll of members of that community. Approval of a *two-state* solution was supported by 65% while only 20% indicated a preference for a *federal state*. This is a substantial reversal of public opinion compared to the 65% vote of Turkish Cypriots supporting the Annan plan in 2004. Apparently, partition is also gathering support among Greek Cypriots. According to a 2006 opinion poll, 48% indicated support for *full* community separation while only 45% still supported reunification. In this sampling, the majority of young Greek Cypriots (63% of ages eighteen to

---

[114] *See* Gul Demir & Niki Gamm, *Rauf Denktas: "Politics Was Not My Choice,"* TURKISH DAILY TIMES, Feb. 3, 2007, http://www.turkishdailynews.com.tr/article.php? enewsid=65303.

twenty-four, and 59% of ages twenty-five to thirty-four) indicated their preference *not* to live with Turkish Cypriots. The irony is that the common ground indicated by the interest in partition from both communities is contrary to the efforts of the international community to bring about reunification of the island, and consistent with this quote attributed to Denktash many years ago: "You cannot force two unwilling partners into marriage."[115]

Meanwhile, at the time when former Greek Cypriot President Papadopoulos still had not decided whether he would run for re-election in 2008, his decision would have an impact on the solution to the Cyprus Problem because of his following actions to that point regarding reunification:[116]

- He proposed demilitarization of the walled capital of Nicosia (the last such divided capital city in the world) so that a crossing point would be opened at the end of one of the city's main commercial streets (Ledra Street) in order to secure safe passage for Cypriots crossing to and from the north through "no man's land."
- He hoped that "during 2007 there would be sufficient preparation for substantive

---

[115] See Lale Sariibrahimoglu, *Two-State Solution for Cyprus?*, TODAY'S ZAMAN, Feb. 1, 2007, http://www.todayszaman.com/tz-web/yazarDetay.do?haberno=101616; *see also Tragic Common Ground Between North and South*, CYPRUS MAIL, http://www.cyprus-mail.com/news/main.php?id=30470&cat_id=1 (last visited Feb. 23, 2007).

[116] *See Cyprus President Against Casino,* FIN. MIRROR, Jan. 18, 2007, http://www.financialmirror.com/more_news.php?id=5854&type=news. "No man's land" is the area of the buffer zone between the two communities patrolled by and under the control of U.N. peacekeeping forces. *See Ibid.*

negotiations leading to a Cyprus settlement."

- He acknowledged that "we know exactly what the other side is aiming at, and they know exactly what we are aiming at. [Turkish Cypriots] clearly want to establish in Cyprus two separate legal entities, upgrade their own entity to a state short of diplomatic recognition . . . . We want a solution that will lead to the reunification of the state, the territory, society, economy, [and] institutions."

- He believed any solution must serve "exclusively" the interests of the Cypriot people.

- He was committed to a bi-zonal, bi-communal federal solution.

- He believed that "people with good will can find a solution without depriving either Greek Cypriots or Turkish Cypriots of their rights."

- He felt that a reunified Cyprus is the "best thing" for Cypriots.

- He stressed that the property issue is "crucial" to a political settlement.

- He felt that there is a better solution than the Annan plan that was rejected by Greek Cypriots in 2004.

- He was "genuinely" in favor of Turkey's European orientation so long as it meets its obligations to the EU and to Cyprus that are the same as required of other candidates for EU membership.

- He did "not want to isolate the Turkish Cypriots" since "it is not in our interest because I think the economic equilibrium is one of the basic necessities, prerequisites for bringing about a solution." But he insisted that

"the issue is not economic but political and figures prove it."
- He continued to oppose opening of the airport in the north to international flights on the ground of "sovereignty of the state."

On the other side, Mehmet Ali Talat (at that time still the Turkish Cypriot leader) had also commented on the Cyprus Problem:[117]

- He wanted more notice from the world for Turkish Cypriots and the lifting of the "unfair isolations" because Turkish Cypriots by their referendum vote "had proved their will for a solution in the island and their intention could not be judged."
- He believed that with the assistance of Turkey, Turkish Cypriots are "striving for" a fair and lasting compromise in Cyprus.
- He noted the "extensive armament in the Greek Cypriot part" and said that this was disconcerting.
- He stated Turkish Cypriots were equal partners with Greek Cypriots in the Republic of Cyprus of 1960 and would be their "political equal" in any future agreement. So they should "have equal right and say on the natural resources on the land and sea areas of the island of Cyprus." This came in response to the argument over who owns the oil in Cyprus and who should receive compensation for it.[118]

---

[117] See Talat: We Want the World to Take Notice of Turkish Cypriots More and Lift the Unfair Isolations, ANATOLIAN TIMES (Turk.), Jan. 23, 2007, http://www.anatoliantimes.com/hbr2.asp?id=160277.
[118] See Talat Letter to Ban Ki-Moon: Turkish Cypriots Have Equal Right on Natural Resources, CYPRUS OBSERVER, Feb. 9, 2007, http://www.observercyprus.com/ observer/NewsDetails.aspx?id=1154.

The United States had also indicated its thoughts on the Cypriot Problem:[119]

- It hoped that "2007 could be a year of Cyprus. And UN Secretary General Ban Ki-Moon is now putting together a team. We hope that there will be even senior Americans on that team in the new UN effort to try to resolve finally the problems that have stemmed from the invasion of Cyprus 30 years ago."

- It was optimistic that 2007 would be the year for a final Cyprus solution based on the "hope that all the relevant parties can come together to once again try to find a solution to this very difficult long-standing problem."

- It felt that ultimately the Greek Cypriots decided against the Annan plan.
- It believed that the region was at "a point now where enough interested parties in the region have expressed an interest in maybe trying again to find a solution."
- It supported renewed UN efforts to find a solution, but the U.S. "would be in a supporting role."

Need to Establish Cooperative Relations

Reed Coughlan considers the 1960 Constitution to have been an uncommon test of consociational democracy doomed to fail from the beginning because Cypriot society lacked the critical element of a third segment where no one of the three was dominant. Cyprus, however, is an ethnic conflict area consisting of "two highly segmented elements…[that] are demographically and economically

---

[119] *See* Sean McCormack, Spokesman, U.S. Dep't of State, Daily Press Briefing (Jan. 10, 2007) (transcript available at http://www.state.gov/r/pa/prs/dpb/2007/78512.htm).

unequal."[120]

After 1974, when the military intervention by Turkey effectively partitioned Cyprus, the possibility of a future federation presented itself through the physical separation resulting from the exchange of populations on the island. However, Coughlan argues that federalism is not a viable solution for Cyprus because the socio-economic inequalities between Greek and Turkish Cypriots have become more acute since the initial experiment during the years 1960-1963. In addition, the island's proximity and importance to both Greece and Turkey have increased the difficulty in resolving the conflict.[121]

Actual bi-communality came into being in the 1570s with the arrival of approximately 20,000 Turkish settlers on the island to join Greeks, Maronites, and Armenians, who numbered around 85,000. When Great Britain accepted control of the island, the approximate split in population was 73.4% "Greek Church" and 24.9% "Mahometan" [of Mohammed]. Over one hundred years have passed since both communities rejected proportional representation because it "would get in the way of exercising what each took to be its legitimate prerogative to dominate the other...[creating a] lack of trust and mutual good will ...[that] persists to this day."[122]

As has been discussed, historically, enosis (unity with Greece) has been sought by Greek Cypriots and

---

[120] *See* Reed Coughlan, *Cyprus: From Corporate Autonomy to the Search for Territorial Federalism, in* AUTONOMY AND ETHNICITY: NEGOTIATING COMPETING CLAIMS IN MULTI-ETHNIC STATES 219, 219-239 (Yash Ghai ed., 2000). Consociational democracy is "the solution to the problem of coexistence inside one single people between different tendencies (religious, social, etc.)."

[121] *Ibid.*

[122] *Ibid.*

opposed by Turkish Cypriots, leading to alienation between the two communities. This has been exacerbated by their distinct educational systems that have perpetuated the historical propaganda of *the other* as enemy through propagandizing the youth on both sides, constantly serving as a reminder of their differences and underscoring historical distrust and antagonism.[123]

The fighting that took place to force the English out of Cyprus had two differing objectives: Greek Cypriots fought for enosis whereas the Turkish Cypriots wanted partition. One of the reasons that the experiment in consociational democracy failed is that there was no such thing as loyalty uniting the two communities. Rather than being one nation as Cypriots with different dispositions, inhabitants of the island were in fact two distinct ethnicities because each considered itself tied to its respective ethnic heritage. And, the leaders of the two communities were not interested in moderation and compromise. This was evident in the pre-independence conflict as well as the post-1960 operation of the fledgling republic. Although the unique aspect of a constitution established to reflect consociational democracy is its recognition of communal separation, the US State Department claimed this to be its great weak point.[124]

The demise of consociational democracy in Cyprus was actually attributable to the composition and structure of the island's society. To succeed, the political leaders of both communities would have been required to commit to the continued unity of the republic and demonstrate a willingness to be flexible and compromise. Because of its dual nature, Cypriot society and its politics created a zero-sum game where the gain by one community was seen as a loss for the other, tending to intensify the intercommunal

---

[123] *Ibid.*

[124] *Ibid.*

hostilities rather than encouraging compromise. Majority segment domination of the minority segment was the result. The dual imbalance proved fatal because Turkish Cypriots were only about 18% of the island's population and also disadvantaged economically. The Greek Cypriot majority deeply resented the agreement to which they became an unwilling party.[125]

The United States, as the primary mediator in the Cyprus conflict, entered the picture in 1963 in order to prevent a war between Greece and Turkey over Cyprus.[126] This intervention had the effect of partitioning the island between the two communities, without taking into consideration the interests and underlying needs of the people. From 1963-1974, the Greek Cypriots pursued a government for the majority that also protected the constitutional rights of the minority. On the other hand, Turkish Cypriots insisted that the constitution provided them with their own separate community with political rights identical to those of Greek Cypriots. By 1974, the de facto partition of the island and the presence of Turkish troops in the north had the dramatic effect of shifting the balance of power so that plans for a federal solution to the Cyprus Problem were severely altered. This has not changed except to demonstrate a hardening of positions.[127]

Greek Cypriots have been successful in internationalizing their position, while Turkish Cypriots have not had the same benefits because the international community (with the exception of Turkey) only recognizes the Greek Cypriot republic. The two communities appear to be moving farther apart as time passes. Greek Cypriots

---

[125] *Ibid.*

[126] *See* Sean J. Byrne, *The Roles of External Ethnoguarantors and Primary Mediators in Cyprus and Northern Ireland*, 24 CONFLICT RESOL. Q. 149, 165 (2006).

[127] *See* Coughlan , *supra* note 120, at 228

want a federation where all powers not specifically designated to the two separate governments are reserved to the central government. Turkish Cypriots see a loose federation where all powers are retained by the two separate states except for those specifically designated to be exercised by the central government. Each side has a different point of view regarding solution to the impasse because both see history in dissimilar ways, while at the same time sharing a bleak view of the future: Insecurity and unwillingness to trust the other. The fundamental conflict between Greek and Turkish Cypriots is about their deep-seated insecurity arising from their respective need for a feeling of safety from the threat each insists is posed by the other side.[128] Both sides are adamant concerning their respective preconditions for negotiation of any settlement. Turkish Cypriots insist on the continued presence of Turkish troops for purposes of their security and safety. Greek Cypriots fear that Turkey is not done concerning its actions commenced in 1974, which could very easily result in a loss of the entire island. Their fears are reinforced by the continued presence of the extremely large contingent of Turkish troops in the north since 1974, resulting in continued Greek Cypriot demands for their withdrawal.[129]

No one can rewrite the history that has resulted in the demand of Greek Cypriots for a strong unitary state and the interest of Turkish Cypriots in a loose confederation. What are the prospects for a bi-communal, bi-zonal federation being the successful resolution of the intractable Cyprus conflict if John Stuart Mills' three conditions to a federation of long duration (i.e., mutual sympathy between the two populations, some degree of mutual need, and assurance that one community will not dominate the other) do not appear to be present in the Cyprus conflict? Mills

---

[128] *Ibid.*

[129] *Ibid.*

would probably conclude that the Cyprus division does not lend itself to a federal solution. Thus what can be done with a conflict that has such a tortured history and the demonstrated ineffectiveness of third party intervention?[130]

There is no recorded history of survival when it comes to a two-unit federation, and where such units are in continual irreconcilable confrontation the eventuality of civil war or secession is great. This is all the more likely where one of the two units is dominant. As bi-communal societies, Northern Ireland, Sri Lanka, and Cyprus face difficulties because the majority communities have succeeded in dominating the minority, making it difficult to design a structure of government that can successfully manage the resulting tensions. In the case of Cyprus, the conflict between Greece and Turkey (as the two "mother countries") has defined the historical struggle.[131]

With the declaration of independence by the Turkish Republic of Northern Cyprus (TRNC) in 1983, following nine years of the island's partition since 1974, it appears that at least de facto independence has been achieved by the Turkish Cypriots. It is not realistic to expect that they will surrender this now and accept federation unwillingly. This is especially true when we consider the history of unsuccessful attempts at international mediation and the conditions required for a successful federation.[132]

The possibility of forgiveness and reconciliation through a restorative justice approach is critical to the consideration of this destructive ethnic conflict. Without this there can be no resolution as forgiveness means relinquishing the drive for vengeance against those who

---

[130] *Ibid.*

[131] *Ibid.*

[132] *Ibid.*

caused harm. An integral element is the willingness to assist in the rehabilitation of the offender without being required to forget the harm suffered. Seeking just punishment is not prohibited so long as the goal is the eventual return of the offender to the community. Forgiveness is preferred over harboring hate so that the parties can move forward with their lives. *The injured party accepts both the good and the bad in themselves as well as in the harm-doer as part of the process of forgiveness.* This does not preclude the victim from establishing conditions of forgiveness that are the subject of the negotiation between harm-doer and victim that is facilitated by an independent impartial intervener from the community. *Beyond forgiveness we find reconciliation that re-establishes the relationship between victim and harm-doer for the future as they move on with their respective lives.* The following are among the issues that are especially important when considering the establishment of cooperative relations in the aftermath of a destructive conflict: [133]

- *Mutual security* by its very nature requires that both sides feel secure so that each side is comfortable. Important to this requirement are disarmament and arms control procedures that are mutually verifiable.

- *Mutual respect* necessarily implies that protection from both physical danger and psychological harm and humiliation requires mutual cooperation. When one side engages in activities such as insult, humiliation, or inconsiderate conduct, the other usually responds in kind. The result is a decrease in

---

[133] *See* Morton Deutsch, *Justice and Conflict, in* THE HANDBOOK OF CONFLICT RESOLUTION: THEORY AND PRACTICE 43, 62-64 (Morton Deutsch et al. eds., 2006).

both physical and psychological security.

- *Humanization of the other* is the antithesis of demonization and requires that each side see the other in the context of everyday activities that emphasize their commonalities rather than their differences.

- *Fair rules for managing conflict* require the preparation for disputes by advance development of all elements for their constructive and just management.

- *Curbing the extremists on both sides* starts with an understanding that when one side initiates extremist conduct within its borders the other side will follow suit so that it becomes necessary for both to act if the effort is to be successful.

- *Gradual development of mutual trust and cooperation* will have the best chance of success if early cooperative endeavors are successful. So the opportunities and projects for cooperative efforts must be: (1) clearly achievable, (2) meaningful, and (3) significant.

Successful prevention of destructive conflict presupposes more than constructive dispute resolution processes. It requires change in the way our societal institutions (economic, educational, familial, political, and religious) recognize and honor human equality, shared community, non-violence, fallibility, and reciprocity. This is how to eliminate gross injustices and at the same time reduce the potential for conflict to become destructive and foster injustice.[134]

Rather than being something that has to lead to war, ethnicity is a social construction of symbols, myths, and

---

[134] *Ibid.*

114

memories that can be changed with the passage of time. While ethnic conflicts have been attributed by some theorists to deep and ancient hatreds or grand clashes of civilizations, it seems that many times the small differences are those that light the fires of antagonism. Although every conflict is different, there is a common dynamic consisting of (1) divisions created by ethnic symbols and myths, and (2) fears for group survival created by economic rivalries or the weakening of state authority. When support is mobilized through appeals to ethnic symbols by elites or leaders, any number of events (such as those of 1963 and 1974 in Cyprus) can spark fighting. The politics of symbolism play a role in the use of the emotional power of ethnic symbols and is used by political entrepreneurs and extremist groups to reconstruct the preferences of the citizenry at large. The result for many ethnic disputes is that they erupt because conflict is preferred over cooperation by one or both sides.[135]

Destructive conflicts persisting for long periods of time are capable of resisting attempts at resolution and may seem to take on a unique life because they attract multiple parties, increase in complication, and threaten what participants feel to be their interests and underlying needs. In conflicts such as the one in Cyprus where hostilities have existed for so long, the results are negative in that they consist of mutual alienation, contempt, and atrocities such as genocide, murder, and rape. The essential point to understand about such unruly conflicts is that they survive precisely because their resolution seems impossible. The persistence, destructiveness, and resistance to resolution of intractable conflicts distinguish them from those that are tractable. If an intractable conflict has persisted for some

---

[135] *See* JOSEPH S. NYE, JR., UNDERSTANDING INTERNATIONAL CONFLICTS: AN INTRODUCTION TO THEORY AND HISTORY 158, 158-161 (Pearson/Longman 2007).

time, many of the following characteristics will be present: (a) context (legacies of dominance and injustice, and instability); (b) issues (human and social polarities, and symbolism and ideology); (c) relationships (exclusive and inescapable, oppositional group identities, and intense internal dynamics); (d) processes (strong emotionality, malignant social processes, and pervasiveness, complexity, and flux); and (e) outcomes (protracted trauma and normalization of hostility and violence).[136]

In addressing intractable conflict there are five major paradigm approaches:[137]

- *Realism.*
- *Human Relations.*
- *Pathology (Medical).*
- *Postmodernism.*
- *Systems.*

There is something in each of these approaches that would be applicable to and useful concerning the Cyprus problem:[138]

- *Realism.* Taking strong protective action.
- *Human Relations.* Re-educating or influencing
- *Pathology.* Considering intractable social conflicts as a disease, infection or cancer that need to be appropriately diagnosed, treated and contained.
- *Postmodern.* Need to change one's view of history.
- *Systems.* Requires that we look at the entire

---

[136] *See* Peter T. Coleman, *Intractable Conflict, in* THE HANDBOOK OF CONFLICT RESOLUTION: THEORY AND PRACTICE 533, 533-555 (Morton Deutsch et al. eds., 2006)

[137] I*bid.*

[138] I*bid.*

116

picture involving the intractable conflict. Thus this appears to be the most applicable to the Cyprus question because of the elements of "mutual security, stability, equality, justice, cooperation, humanization of the other, reconciliation, tolerance of difference, containment of tension and violence, compatibility and complexity of meaning, healing, and reconstruction...that may produce a sustained pattern of transformational change."[139]

What, then, should be the guidelines for intervention in Cyprus? Looking to the work of Morton Deutsch, Dean Pruitt, Paul Olczak, Heidi Burgess, Guy Burgess, John Paul Lederach, Herbert Kelman, and Michael Wessells, we can consider the following:[140] Conducting a thorough analysis of the conflict system prior to intervention; considering the complexity of intractable conflict, a multidisciplinary framework must include a foundation based on analysis and intervention; fostering an authentic experience of "ripeness" among disputants or key representatives of the various groups involved in an intractable conflict;[141] orienting the disputants toward the primary objective of defining a fair, constructive process of conflict engagement rather than attempting to achieve

---

[139] *Ibid.*

[140] *Ibid.*

[141] *Ibid.* at 549-551. This is "one of the first and most critical challenges conflict resolvers face when working with malignant conflict systems" because the disputants must be helped "to cross their own social psychological barriers to making peace with their enemy." *Ibid.* "When destructive and escalatory dynamics have become normalized, ripeness should be viewed as a commitment to a *change* in the nature of the relations of the parties from a destructive orientation toward a more constructive state of coexistence with potential for mutual gain." *Ibid.*

117

conflict resolution outcomes; using elicitive (rather than prescriptive) approaches when working across cultures;[142] using short-term interventions such as crisis management that are coordinated and mindful of long-term objectives; and initiating and sustaining constructive, nonlinear change.[143] Appropriate approaches for issues rooted in the past, the present, and the future must be integrated in the general intervention strategy. In the end, success is directly tied to a greater ability to understand the power of the past while possessing the patience and tolerance demanded for the practice of effective dispute resolution skills in such circumstances. Although many attempts are made to resolve conflict situations, only a few

[142] *Ibid.* at 551-552. This tends to be both more respectful of disputants and more empowering and sustainable. *Ibid.* A prescriptive intervenor is one who is perceived as the expert while the participants are "passive recipients of predetermined knowledge, models, and skills" of the intervenor. *Ibid.* at 552. The elicitive approach emphasizes "the local, cultural expertise of the participants" so both intervenor and participants "together design interventions that are specifically suited to the problems, resources, and constraints of the specific cultural context." *Ibid.* An elicitive approach eliminates the bias embraced by prescriptive intervention but additionally empowers the participants through respect for, embracing of, and accommodating their voices.

[143] *Ibid.* at 553-554. Effects of three impact types are possible: (1) *episodic* ("direct and immediate but typically short term or superficial"); (2) *developmental* (takes time to unfold but may greatly affect the quality of the patterns of the interaction); and (3) *radical* (dramatic alteration of the system's pattern). *Ibid.* at 554. The "agent of change" level can also result in categorical differences in the initiatives of change themselves. *Ibid.* There are three general agent of change levels: (1) *top-down* ("leaders and elite decision makers"); (2) *middle-out* ("key midlevel leaders and community networks and structures"); and (3) *bottom-up* ("grassroots organizations or the masses directly"). *Ibid. Radical* impact from the *bottom-up* seems to have the best chance of succeeding to "trigger fundamental shifts in conflict patterns (from destructive to constructive) through small but important changes" that are *"frame-breaking." Ibid.*

are successful.[144] The main indication for possible settlement is "ripeness," which translates into that point where both sides are "hurting" so much that the cost to continue is too great (the "hurting stalemate" concept).[145] Not all hurting stalemate situations have led to settlement, Cyprus being a prime example.[146]

Today, the Cyprus conflict still remains an enigma in the arena of international conflict. In close to half a century, UN peacemaking efforts have yielded only two agreements in the 1970s that aspired to a bi-communal federation. Yet even these efforts have been undermined by mistrust between the two communities, creating a de facto political division of the island. As long as this mistrust continues, no proposal – however well-crafted –will mend the situation. A possible prerequisite to creating a united Cyprus is the acknowledgement of the political as well as psychological underpinning of the division that has survived for at least two generations. This requires acknowledgement that there are in fact two *equal* political communities existing on the island so that each will feel secure to do what is necessary to establish friendly relations with the other. One of the key roadblocks is in the word "equal." Although the 1960 Constitution of the Republic of Cyprus was bi-communal in nature, it served to deepen the divisions between the two communities. The constitution did not establish a shared Cypriot identity, but perpetuated distrust by maintaining a delicate balance between the respective interests of the Greek majority and Turkish minority. To worsen matters, it contained "remnants of

---

[144] *See* HUGH MIALL ET AL., CONTEMPORARY CONFLICT RESOLUTION 162 (1st ed. 1999).

[145] *Ibid.* This may "foster great commitment to the peace process" by the participants ultimately leading "to plans and initiatives with prolonged sustainability."

[146] *Ibid.*

119

colonial rule that could not be resolved on independence and were thus left to be worked out by the Cypriots themselves."[147]

The 1960 Constitution contained the following characteristics of a power-sharing system: (1) coalition of major ethnic groups, (2) proportional allocation of public service appointments and funds, (3) segmental autonomy, and (4) decision-making subject to mutual veto; however, there was a failure of power-sharing on the island. This failure resulted from four elements: (1) lack of fairness, (2) lack of functionality, (3) lack of political will, and (4) lack of common identity. After only three years dealing with the constitution, Makarios attempted to secure its revision to remove obstacles interpreted by the Greek Cypriots to be detrimental to the functional operation of the government, which itself resulted in an aftermath that "left Cyprus *de facto* partitioned."[148]

Greek Cypriots have sought a federal republic that would (1) be independent, (2) maintain territorial unity, (3) recognize a single sovereignty, and (4) provide the same citizenship for all Cypriots. They have strived to achieve a 70:30 ratio in elected representation and a reduction of the Turkish Cypriot area to facilitate repatriation of at least a majority of the 160,000 Greek Cypriot refugees to their homes in the north. They have also demanded unrestricted freedom of movement, residence, and property. Additionally, they insist on the complete demilitarization of the island and "repatriation" of Turkish settlers who have immigrated to the north since 1974. Turkish Cypriots have sought to emphasize the bi-zonal, bi-communal aspects of a

---

[147] Susanne Baier-Allen, *The Failure of Power-Sharing in Cyprus: Causes and Consequences*, in MANAGING AND SETTLING ETHNIC CONFLICTS 77, 77-91, 262-280 (Ulrich Schneckener & Stefan Wolff eds., 2004). (emphasis added)

[148] *Ibid.*

new federal republic with each separate community having equal partnership status. Any such new federal republic would hold powers limited to the following equally represented areas: foreign affairs, finance, and economic coordination. The two separate constituent states would retain all other powers. Only minor concessions would be made so that Turkish Cypriots would retain at least twenty-nine percent of the territory on the island. They feel that the three freedoms advanced by the Greek Cypriots should be restricted, especially to the right to acquire property where compensation should be the method of adjustment. In the eyes of Turkish Cypriots neither the presence of mainlanders from Turkey or Turkish troops is an issue for negotiation. Since they see both communities as equal they insist that sovereignty should be treated in like manner. While Greek Cypriots have officially supported a federal solution when facing international observation, domestically their political leaders have rejected the proposal as an acknowledgment of "defeat" in the 1974 war. On the other hand, although Turkish Cypriots have promoted a two-state confederation in an effort to preserve their 1974 gains, Turkey has been the only outside supporter of this two-state proposal. And, at the end of the day, the international community has pushed not for a confederation, but a bi-zonal, bi-communal federation.[149]

As the world's ethnic conflicts have become more visible, academic circles have begun to embrace the ideas of secession and partition. Consequently, the future of a possible federal solution in Cyprus has been seriously questioned. Both sides seem to prefer the status quo to accepting the suggestions of the other. Although continuation of the status quo over the long run seems to be a situation that is unsettled and volatile, the international community is faced with a troubling dilemma. Partition

---

[149] *Ibid.*

121

violates international law if it is not by mutual agreement, and a federal solution cannot be imposed because lack of public support would doom it from the beginning. While there have been threats that UN peacekeepers would be withdrawn in the event of indefinite continuation of the status quo, this likely would result in a void potentially leading to armed conflict. And, diplomatic withdrawal would succeed in simply leaving the Cypriots on their own without the resolve to work toward a negotiated solution.[150]

Susanne Baier-Allen has suggested that moving beyond the status quo will require certain elements of the current division to be accepted, namely existence of the two separate ethnic communities, each controlling politically their own administration. Acknowledgement of the current state of affairs in Cyprus is also necessary as a precondition to establishing the trust required to continue the negotiation process. Additionally, she believes political and economic confidence-building measures are needed. Her approach to restarting the negotiation process requires an understanding that a solution will not result from hammering out another constitutional structure, albeit through discussions designed to reach agreement. In the long term, she feels that a solution must start with an understanding of the psychological mind set of *ordinary citizens as well as officials*, with the goal of changing negative perceptions of the other side in favor of positive impressions. This means that those who will have to live with the outcome must be the starting point. Interestingly, Baier-Allen predicts that a failure by the EU to use the "carrot and stick" approach to get the parties to compromise would be fatal. "If the EU simply accepted a divided Cyprus, then the Green Line would become one of its external borders, cementing the division of the island."[151]

---

[150] *Ibid.*

[151] *Ibid.* (emphasis added).

122

Nonetheless, on May 1, 2004, the EU accepted a divided Cyprus.

Challenges and Future Opportunities

Peace has been "spoiled" in Cyprus since the inter-communal fighting of 1963 and the following partition of the island in 1974. To further exacerbate the problem, each community has taken actions that have strengthened their respective positions at the expense of the other's basic needs. The failure of the UN to succeed in mediating the conflict is attributable to the spoiling activities of different actors advocating the specific bargaining positions of the two communities. Spoiling is not a clear-cut action, but rather differs from "normal politics" by a matter of degree. In Cyprus, this phenomenon has not been inimical to negotiation processes but rather to the peace process and settlement of the conflict. Spoiling has been accomplished by those who have believed that a particular vision of a future Cyprus was attainable. While spoiling contains its own ideology and perceptions of power, responsibility must also be shared by vested interests in ending the conflict. The relatively low turnover of political elites in each community has accentuated this problem by reducing the potential for meaningful change and prevented a real transformation of interests and underlying needs, and the open discussion required to accomplish this. The basic needs of the principal parties and the "spoiling" positions and actions they have advanced to satisfy such requirements are numerous.[152] Greek Cypriots want:

- Reunification of Cyprus and

---

[152] Nathalie Tocci, *Spoiling Peace in Cyprus, in* CHALLENGES TO PEACEBUILDING: MANAGING SPOILERS DURING CONFLICT RESOLUTION 262, 262-280 (Edward Newman & Oliver Richmond eds., 2006).

avoidance of secession by the northern part of the island or its annexation to Turkey.

- A return to the status quo prior to the 1974 arrival of Turkish mainland troops and the larger territorial share and political representation.
- Liberalization of the "three freedoms" (movement, settlement, and property) as well as respect for human rights, including the right of refugees to return to their properties in the north.
- Security guarantees against Turkish aggression.
- Abrogation of the Treaty of Guaranty of 1959, replacing those unilateral rights of intervention in Cyprus by Britain, Greece, and Turkey with international guarantees that would prevent Turkey from interfering in the affairs of the island.
- Complete repatriation of Turkish immigrants who came to Cyprus after 1974.

On the other hand, Turkish Cypriots want:

- Political equality with Greek Cypriots.
- Continued Turkish security guarantees.
- Rigid limitations on the number of Greek Cypriots allowed to return to the north and the time frame for that to occur, as well as insisting that reciprocal property claims be resolved mostly through

124

compensation and inter-communal property exchanges.

The reason that the foregoing assertions are considered as "spoiling" rather than simply political positions in the normal course of human interaction is because they effectively inhibit the attainment of the respective interests and underlying needs of each community. Over the years, both parties have attempted to legitimize their spoiling positions in various ways. Since 1974, the Greek Cypriots have been persuaded by the government, civil society, and the media of the moral and legal superiority of their cause. Certain factions have also characterized any attempt by the Greek government to pressure Greek Cypriots to a settlement, as a betrayal of the Greek Cypriots and an abdication of Greece's responsibilities as their mother country.[153] Turkish Cypriots have played upon fears of renewed domination by Greek Cypriots, as the main argument to support independent statehood. As a result, Turkish Cypriots see the return of Greek Cypriot refugees, the liberalization of the "three freedoms," or intercommunal contact as a return to the unacceptable status quo ante 1963. Concerns about displacement through property readjustments and the repatriation of Turkish settlers have also served as justification for their spoiling positions. To further complicate matters, Turkey has insisted that Cyprus is the key to Turkish national security and necessary to protect it from potential Greek aggression. Spoiling has been enabled by international third parties. Greek Cypriots have enlisted the aid of the UN, EU, and the European Court of Human Rights (ECHR), while Turkish Cypriots have "mirrored" the actions of Greek Cypriots. With increased success for the Greek Cypriots coming from the international community, the Turkish Cypriots stepped up

---

[153] *Ibid. at 273.*

125

their insistence on political equality conditioned by recognition of their sovereignty. Turkish and Turkish Cypriot nationalists even argued that unilateral admission of Greek Cypriots to the EU without Turkish Cypriots and the prior admission of Turkey would lead to permanent partition of the island.[154]

The EU's potential for generating support for reunification was a missed opportunity through the failure to foster a new effort to build consensus among all elements on the island, resulting in increased spoiling arguments and tactics. The current situation is ripe for further spoiling because EU membership for Greek Cypriots places them in an improved bargaining position to prevent further EU actions that could assist the Turkish Cypriots by lifting the restrictions causing their international isolation. Also, the unintentional actions of the EU in allowing the possibility of full membership for a divided Cyprus has encouraged the efforts of Turkish and Turkish Cypriot nationalists in arguing that this could consolidate partition. The ultimate reversal occurred when the people in the north forced moderation through a positive referendum vote – but that went for naught because the Greek Cypriot spoilers carried the day. Finally, the EU's inability to create an effective policy regarding Turkey missed the opportunity to cause a change in Turkey's policy towards Cyprus prior to the Turkish elections in November 2002. The principal lesson here is that the EU's unsuccessful policies in Cyprus are its "failure to account for the diverse make-up of the parties in the conflict...[through lack of] a common and consistent EU foreign policy towards the conflict [that] never

---

[154] *Ibid.* at 272, 277. Notably, the desirability of true compromise with the Turkish Cypriots has never been advanced by the political class. *Ibid.* at 273.

materialized."[155]

As was mentioned earlier, in order to achieve a mediated result similar to that reached in South Africa, there must be a stalemate that is mutually hurting. However, the hurting stalemate in Cyprus is not mutual because the Greek Cypriots appear to be able to do quite well without the Turkish Cypriots, especially after Greek Cypriot admission to the EU. The reverse appears not to be true for the Turkish Cypriots. For successful peacebuilding in Cyprus there must be "an intersection of the objectives, the actors, and a complementarity of the mediators' [primary and external ethno guarantors] roles and their functions."[156]

How to Work With This Conflict

In working with a system of intractable conflict, we need to understand the interrelationship of the inter-communal elements and their interaction with outside influences as they change with the passage of time. This will require a consideration of the positive and negative feedback that may result in escalation, de-escalation, and stabilization of the dispute. The complex activities utilized would be in the nature of integrating varied viewpoints and method systems that will deal with goals of an immediate, short-term and long-term nature, in an organized fashion, while considering the distinctions between the past, present, and future intervention approaches. "Ripeness" is also a critical element in the process. Emphasizing the introduction of forces of change rather than removal of

---

[155] *Ibid.*

[156] *See* Byrne, *supra* note 126, at 163. The third-party interveners in the conflicts existing in Cyprus and Northern Ireland are of two types: Primary mediators are those "who have the power and clout to enforce agreements," and regional external ethnoguarantors are those "who have cultural, historical, and political ties to internal allies."

127

obstacles of resistance, it is crucial to determine the present commitment of the conflicting parties to participate in a conflict process that is constructive rather than destructive. Following closely is the requirement of awareness of post-traumatic stress syndrome symptoms and manifestations of trauma at the community level, as well as knowledge of crisis intervention in cases of emergency.[157]

Constructive conflict processes require the use of collaborative alternative dispute resolution forms of independent/neutral third-party intervention plus facilitation of dialogue sessions, town hall meetings, problem-solving and other confidence-building workshops. Elicitation of locally relevant cross-cultural information is also important. Because it is necessary to intervene at an early point when the parties to a conflict are able to "still see the humanity and the validity of the other's needs...[the] greatest hope in working intractable conflicts is to find the means to avert them."[158] In the case of the long-standing Cyprus Problem it is far too late to avert the conflict. The question is whether it is too late to intervene successfully with a new creative approach.

De Jure Partition May be Likely Solution

It is perilous to ignore intractable conflict.[159] The role of emotions indicates that simply working to "separate the people from the problem and focus on interests instead of positions to surface options for mutual gain that . . . will be embraced by all" has limited applicable success to

---

[157] *See* Coleman, *supra* note 136, at 556 (referring to dynamical system theory as applied to the Cyprus problem).

[158] *Ibid.* at 557.

[159] Heidi Burgess, Guy Burgess & Sandra Kaufman, *The Challenge of Intractable Conflicts: Introduction to the Colloquium*, 24 CONFLICT RESOL. Q. 173, 174 (2006).

intractable conflict (although both sides of the Cyprus Problem have many commonalities).[160] The Cyprus conflict is intractable because it has proved an unworthy candidate for mediation. While not hopeless, it is arguable that success can only be accomplished through transforming it into a more peaceful and cooperative situation than has been the case to date. This transformation will ensure that the parties will live side-by-side peacefully while they continue to disagree. At some point, perhaps they will once again approach the bargaining table to reconsider reunification. Until that time, transformation of the relationship between the two communities will help to establish stability in the region.

For such a transformation to take place, outside third parties who have mismanaged the problem will need to withdraw. The only sure way to avoid mismanagement by third parties would be for the people themselves on both sides of the dispute, and at the grassroots level, to take control of their own destiny. This can be accomplished through transforming "the culture of the conflict into a culture of peace" that empowers the citizenry on both sides "in a constructive conflict-resolution process" through use of "storytelling and dialogue groups," enabling the parties to "mourn, heal, reconcile, and forge a new constructive story."[161] Failing this, "future seeds of destruction may be sown for the next generation to deal with."[162]

In December 2005, Turkish Cypriots constructed a bridge in the divided capital city of Nicosia to ease movement for Turkish troops stationed in the north. This

---

[160] *See ibid.* at 175.

[161] *See* Byrne, *supra* note 126, at 167. Storytelling is used to surface "underlying complexities in virulent protracted conflict situations" and can be used "as an intervention to build bridges between communities." *Ibid.*

[162] *Ibid.*

129

upset Greek Cypriots and frustrated plans for constructing a new crossing point at the Ledra Street boundary in the middle of the divided capital.[163] In January 2007, Turkish Cypriots extended a reconciliation gesture by starting to dismantle the bridge.[164] On March 9, 2007, Greek Cypriots, in a reciprocal good faith gesture, demolished a dividing wall on the Ledra boundary street.[165]

Complicating the situation was a then recent statement by a Turkish academic that UN Peacekeeping Forces are no longer needed in Cyprus because the division of the island "into two distinct states" has eliminated "any cause for conflict between the two communities."[166] The academic added: "The intricate and chronic Cyprus issue has caused a waste of time and resources."[167] Moreover, an important Greek Cypriot columnist has commented: "In short, after 44 years, during which there were countless rounds of negotiations and all aspects of a settlement agreed, apart from a few points that were completed by the UN at Bürgenstock, we now want everything deleted and to start from scratch. At best, at this rate, we might hope for a

---

[163] *Ibid.*; *see also A Timeline of Key Events in Cyprus' History,* INT'L HERALD TRIB., Mar. 9, 2007, http://www.iht.com/articles/ap/2007/03/09/europe/EU-GEN-Cyprus-Timeline.php.

[164] *Ibid.*

[165] *Ibid.*; *but see Cyprus' Greek Side Razes Part of Barrier,* L.A. TIMES, Mar. 9, 2007, at A9, *available at* LEXIS (reporting that the Greek Cypriot President Tassos Papadopoulos had said that there would be no civilian crossing where that checkpoint had been until Turkey removed its troops from the location).

[166] *See* Ali Aslan Kilic, *Experts Suggest Removal of UN Peacekeeping Force in Cyprus,* TODAY'S ZAMAN, Mar. 10, 2007, http://www.todayszaman.com/tz-web/detaylar.do?load=detay&link=105048.

[167] *Ibid.*

Cyprus settlement in 50 years from today."[168] He suggested that the two leaders of the respective communities might better serve the peace process if they spent the afternoon together in the northern village of Kyrenia.[169] In doing so, "they would finally realize [sic] that they solved the Cyprus problem, for good, in 2004 and did not have to exert themselves [any further] . . . in order to achieve their objective. The objective has already been achieved."[170] Presumably he was referring to the de facto partition informally recognized by the results of the April 2004 referenda vote.

A prominent Turkish columnist has also indicated that the "single state model" will no longer work,[171] and "behind closed doors" there is a possibility for a "negotiated partition of the island" because of the failure to provide equal status for both communities.[172] "Despite insistence on putting efforts on plans for the unity of the island, in the coming years we may be hearing increased

---

[168] See Loucas Charalambous, *Return to Point Zero*, CYPRUS MAIL, http://www.cyprus-mail.com/news/main.php?id=31087&cat_id=1 (last visited Mar. 6, 2007). Secretary-General Kofi Annan arrived on Saturday March 27, 2004, in Bürgenstock, Switzerland, where talks involving the Greek Cypriot and Turkish Cypriot parties, with the participation of Greece and Turkey, were underway. Secretary-General's Visit to Burgenstock, Switzerland (March 28-31, 2004), http://www.un.org/av/ photo/sgtrips/sgswitz032804.htm (last visited Apr. 28, 2007). On Monday, March 29, 2004, the Secretary-General unveiled a revised Cyprus plan that he said would "break the ice" in stalled reunification talks. *Ibid.*

[169] *Ibid.*

[170] *Ibid.*

[171] See Lale Sariibrahimoglu, *Negotiated Partition: An Ideal Solution for Cyprus*, TODAY'S ZAMAN, Mar. 6, 2007, http://www.todayszaman.com/tz-web/yazarDetay.do? haberno=104603.

[172] *Ibid.*

voices in public for a negotiated partition process as any attempt to unite the island is becoming outdated. We can't change the natural flow of the river, can we?"[173]

Is it too late to intervene successfully in the Cyprus conflict with a new creative approach? The answer would seem to be "yes" unless we alter the game by applying a *radical* change initiative from the *bottom-up* level through organization of inter-communal grassroots dialogue workshop groups that will: (1) strive to "see the humanity and the validity of the other's needs"[174] and (2) follow up the workshops with education and mobilization of their respective communities as *Cypriots* to make known their desire for reunification at the polls. Among other issues, these workshops would consider mutual security, mutual respect, humanization of the other, fair rules for managing conflict, curbing the extremists on both sides, and gradual development of mutual trust and cooperation.

The different priorities of the two communities may make it possible for each to achieve their goals without harming the other. Being able to work well with conflict will strengthen how they relate to each other and provide opportunities to deal with their differences, thereby turning opponents into collaborators. This means converting the immediate goal of the *reason* we deal with the other side to one where we improve the *method* of dealing with them, so our focus on process leads us to the same side of the table. This requires that we change our approach and ask *different questions* than those propounded in the past. Conflicting interests can be handled more successfully in this manner. The issue is about how we deal with conflicting *views* rather than asserting rights, assessing wrong, or laying blame, and the *method* we use for future changes that are sure to come. One side asking itself *what* it would like the

---

[173] *Ibid.*

[174] *See* Coleman, *supra* note 136, at 557.

132

other side to do, *why* the other side has failed to follow through, and *how* it could aid the other side in doing so, is a good starting place as long as this process is mutual so that all points of view are honored. Nevertheless, each side needs to change the questions that it has been asking of the other.[175]

Some of this has been occurring through efforts funded from the outside, such as the 2005 bi-communal advanced narrative mediation workshop in Nicosia and the 2006 bi-communal workshop for Cypriot academics in San Diego, California (both programs were conducted by John Winslade, Gerald Monk, and myself), with financial support from the Fred J. Hansen Institute for World Peace at San Diego State University. In addition, the 2006-2007 Rock Rose Institute Youth Dialogue Project (YDP) engaged youths aged eighteen to twenty-four from five countries including Cyprus "based on their role as change makers in their communities and their ongoing commitment to non-violence."[176] Also, human rights efforts should be made in both communities to establish "truth and reconciliation" type groups. But the grassroots on both sides must become vocal in their *bottom-up* support, as well as participation and advocacy, because "any solution will have to be put to the test by *the people* that have to live with it. . .any solution has to start *with them*."[177]

Failing this, it would seem that the future holds little promise for reunification. As it becomes evident from a world view that the independence of Kosovo may be possible, the Greek Cypriot administration "is becoming increasingly concerned" about the possibility of such a precedent assisting the Turkish Cypriots in a like

---

[175] *See* ROGER FISHER ET AL., BEYOND MACHIAVELLI 143,144 (Harvard Univ. Press 1994).

[176] *See* Appendix E.

[177] Baier-Allen, *supra* note 147, at 91 (emphasis added).

133

manner.[178] In the event of a similar occurrence, a de jure partition of Cyprus may be the likely solution.

---

[178] Selcuk Gültali, *Greek Cypriots Fear Kosovo May Set Precedent for Northern Cyprus*, TODAY'S ZAMAN, Mar. 20, 2007, http://www.todayszaman.com/tz-web/detaylar.do?load=detay&link=105722.

III

CYPRUS AND TRADITIONAL SPOILING[179]

Nothing Changes by Dealing with the Past

We now examine the current view of the problem, consider Cyprus as an example of traditional spoiling in the negotiation culture of lengthy peace processes, explore the absence of civil society representation at the bargaining table as a negative impact on the potential for settlement, evaluate suggestions for an approach to management of the pre-negotiation process to effectively facilitate the positive outcome of subsequent negotiations, and conclude that the best hope for reunification of the island of Cyprus rests at the grassroots level in the hands of the people on both sides, who need to change the game through conflict transformation from the bottom-up. To recap, by the time the late 1990s arrived:[180]

- Approximately more than 50% of the TRNC population consisted of "settlers" (immigrants) from Turkey in addition to the estimated 35,000 Turkish soldiers.
- For the first time since 1974, the year 2001 saw the two leaders (Turkish Cypriot Rauf Denktash and Greek Cypriot Glafkos Clerides) meet for dinner in the south, "an unheard of, landmark event," signaling what

---

[179] *See* A. Marco Turk. 2009. "The Negotiation Culture of Lengthy Peace Processes: Cyprus as an Example of Spoiling that Prevents a Final Solution." LOY. L.A. INT'L & COMP. L. REV. 31:327-362.

[180] STEVEN D. STRAUSS, THE COMPLETE IDIOT'S GUIDE TO WORLD CONFLICTS 219, 219-222 (2002). NOTE: Some of this information has been updated through corrections received from Mustafa Akinci, former Mayor of North Nicosia and TRNC Minister of Tourism, on June 3, 2013 (on file with author).

after 25 years could be significant progress toward a possible solution to the deadlock.[181]

- With the arrival of 2003, the Green Line checkpoint was opened so that Cypriots could go back-and-forth between the two communities.[182]
- Yet, by 2004, while Turkish Cypriots voted 65% (64.9%) to approve the Annan Plan and reunification; Greek Cypriots voted 76% (75.8%) against it.[183]
- Currently, no mutually acceptable resolution has been achieved, nor have any new proposals been established to improve conditions for mutual understanding.

Greece, Turkey and Cyprus create a "triangle of conflict" as well as opportunity.[184] There has been a

---

[181] *Ibid.* at 221-222. Potential impetus for the meeting appears to have been European Union (EU) membership for Cyprus on the horizon, possible damage to Turkey's own EU membership hopes if a divided island were admitted to the EU while Turkey was "an occupying power," and the questionable desire of Denktash to reach a settlement before he would retire from office in 2005 at the age of 81. Following the dinner, an enthusiastic Turkish Foreign Minister, Ismail Cem, proclaimed that, "[a] mutually acceptable resolution should be achieved before the end of 2002. We have a new platform which has created improved conditions for mutual understanding." NOTE: Some of this information has been updated through corrections received from Mustafa Akinci, former Mayor of North Nicosia and TRNC Minister of Tourism, on June 3, 2013 (on file with author).

[182] HARRY ANASTASIOU, THE BROKEN OLIVE BRANCH: NATIONALISM, ETHNIC CONFLICT, AND THE QUEST FOR PEACE IN CYPRUS. V.2 NATIONALISM VERSUS EUROPEANIZATION 72 (2008), http://digilib.syr.edu/u?/su-press.

[183] *Ibid.* at 139.

[184] *See generally* GREECE, TURKEY, CYPRUS: TRIANGLE OF CONFLICT – AND OPPORTUNITY 1 (Richard Buckley, ed. 1998)

136

troubled history of this relationship, but the problem created by the Cyprus division caused an escalation in the tension that frustrated all attempts by the international community to achieve a settlement. How the problem can be resolved remains a mystery. Greece and the Republic of Cyprus have a mutual defense agreement, but Turkey and the self-proclaimed Turkish Republic of Northern Cyprus do not. Turkey justifies her presence under the terms of the Treaty of Guarantee.[185] Each side of the dispute remains resistant to movement and the status quo appears to be interminable, unless war or a cooperative change in approach occurs. Since 1963, discussions concerning the Cyprus Problem have centered on extensive political analysis of the division and the consistent efforts to categorize each failed opportunity as being at "a critical stage" in the negotiation process.[186] For more than a quarter century, the UN has unsuccessfully attempted to achieve settlement of this increasingly intractable conflict, but nothing seems to have worked.[187] The only apparent result

[hereinafter TRIANGLE OF CONFLICT – AND OPPORTUNITY] (arguing that all three countries would suffer greatly from an escalation of conflict and benefit enormously from reconciliation). NOTE: Some of this information has been updated through corrections received from Mustafa Akinci, former Mayor of North Nicosia and TRNC Minister of Tourism, on June 3, 2013 (on file with author).

[185] NOTE: Some of this information has been updated through corrections received from Mustafa Akinci, former Mayor of North Nicosia and TRNC Minister of Tourism, on June 3, 2013 (on file with author).

[186] *See, e.g.,* Niyazi Kizilyurek, *Cyprus Silently Begins Year 2009*, CYPRUS OBSERVER, Jan. 9, 2009, http://www.observercyprus.com/observer/NewsDetails.aspx?id=3382#.

[187] *See* Zenon Stavrinides, *The Underlying Assumptions, Structure and Prospects of the Negotiating Process for a Cyprus Settlement, in* PROCEEDINGS OF THE SIXTH INTERNATIONAL CONGRESS OF CYPRESS [sic] STUDIES 69, 69-98 (Ulker Vanci Osam, ed. 2008).

137

is a regular "digging in of the heels" from both sides as their respective positions become more hardened with the passage of time. This has resulted in a period "where groups and the public have no enthusiasm for a solution."[188] So long as the leaders of both sides (now Turkish Cypriot Dervis Eroglu and Greek Cypriot Demetris Christofias) deal with the same issues of the past ("dead junk") as the way to a solution "rather than bring people together," nothing will change.[189]

Another Look at the Problem

In response to my suggestion for a "bottom-up" approach rather than a continuation of the traditional political elite "top-down" method, it has been said that the objectives of Christofias and Talat were reflective of the interests and underlying needs of the majority of the people on both sides of the Green Line that divides the two communities. Further, if "ordinary" Greek and Turkish Cypriots were to meet and begin negotiating a settlement, it was assumed they would start where those two leaders were toiling. This is based on the belief that, as was the case with their predecessors, those two and their respective community establishments had the political acumen and realistic expectations to conclude that current negotiations would not produce the desired results, in view of the military and diplomatic elements on the island. Yet, it was presumed that Christofias and Talat believed they could achieve an agreement that would be preferable to the then present circumstances as well as be supported by "clear majorities in their communities."[190] However, the

---

[188] Kizilyurk, *supra* note 186.

[189] *Ibid.*

[190] *See* E-mail from Dr. Zenon Stravrinides, School of Politics and International Studies, University of Leeds (Sept. 22, 2008) (on file with author).

138

subsequent change in Turkish Cypriot leadership has hardened the division. There must be resolution on many issues that divide the two communities and on which they still stand far apart. Not the least of these is the following list:[191]

- Creation of a power-sharing formula that each can accept and with which each will be comfortable and secure.
- Removal of those settlers (immigrants) from Turkey who have increasingly populated the island since 1974.
- Freedom of movement, settlement, and property ownership throughout the island by both communities.
- Compensation for property losses resulting from division of the island.
- Right of return to property owned on the other side.
- Searching and accounting for missing persons.
- Recognition of pre-partition injustices committed by each community against the other.
- Security concerns harbored by each community regarding the other (e.g., Greek Cypriots unease over the continued presence of Turkish troops and Turkish Cypriot fears of once again becoming the minority on a reunified island).
- Whether to use the most recent version of the Annan Plan as the basis to restart

---

[191] While the reunification debate could encompass other issues, these are the ones that appear with regularity when discussions occur concerning possible solutions to the Cyprus Problem.

139

negotiations or find some other basis (Greek Cypriots wanting nothing to do with the plan at all, and Turkish Cypriots preferring to start from that document).

Each community has its own perception of the problem, its origin, and how to properly and justly settle it.[192] Perhaps this difference in outlook has its roots in the long history of the island's occupation or semi-occupation (excepting only the years 1960-1974) by non-Cypriots, approaching 830 years. Beginning in 1963, fulfillment of the basic needs of each community has been "spoiled" by internal and external forces. On one side, there are the Greek Cypriots convinced of the superiority of the cause they espouse; on the other, there are the Turkish Cypriots who harbor fears of once again being dominated by the other community and a return of the unacceptable status quo that favored the Greek Cypriots in 1963. Making an accommodation even more difficult are issues such as increasing construction on Greek Cypriot land in the Turkish Cypriot community for use by non-Greek Cypriots, repatriation to Turkey of the approximately 250,000 Turkish settlers/immigrants on the island, the claim by Turkey that Cyprus is an imperative consideration regarding Turkey's security, and the Turkish Cypriot indication that it would be a good idea to break up the island and begin again.[193]

The large majority of Greek Cypriots believe that they were wronged by the arrival of Turkish troops in 1974 and their continued presence on the northern portion of the island that Turkish Cypriots still control. Greek Cypriots

---

[192] *See* Stavrinides, *supra* note 187.

[193] *See* A. Marco Turk, *Is Cypriot Unification Possible?* NEW STATESMAN, Aug. 19, 2008, *available at* http://www.newstatesman.com/europe/2008/08/cyprus-conflict-cypriots.

want the troops removed and the island returned, to the extent possible, to its geographical and political status before it was altered in 1974. In addition, they want guarantees that this will not occur again.[194] On the other hand, Turkish Cypriots believe that the problem was created far earlier than 1974. According to them, it was the result of the 1963-1964 inter-communal disruption that reduced the Turkish Cypriots to minority status in the course of Greek Cypriot efforts to unite with Greece. Turkish Cypriots will not agree to return to their earlier minority status, nor will they accept withdrawal of Turkish troops in the absence of a negotiated *bi-zonal, bi-communal federation* supported internationally. Such an arrangement that would have established two separate states under the umbrella of a federal government capable of representing the island internationally was approved by Turkish Cypriots, but rejected by Greek Cypriots at the April 24, 2004, referenda voting.[195] While Greek Cypriots have not been successful in obtaining international or third-party support for removal of the Turkish troops, neither have the Turkish Cypriots been able to succeed in getting any country other than Turkey to recognize and deal with them under the current circumstances.[196] The structure of the negotiations that took place between 1975 and 2004 can be examined in terms of various "underlying assumptions." These include:[197]

- Each side desires to obtain that to which it feels it has a right.
- No concern is exhibited for what is mutually beneficial.

---

[194] *See* Stavrinides, *supra* note 187.

[195] *Ibid.* at 70.

[196] *Ibid.*

[197] *Ibid* at 77-78.

- A *zero-sum*[198] bargaining approach is taken.
- Neither community is willing to relinquish certain advantages obtained by them as a result of the division.

Greek Cypriots must decide between insisting on how Greek they want the Republic of Cyprus, a stable and strong economy with its high standard of living, the reality of slogans for struggle and justice, or a bi-zonal, bi-communal federal republic that will require equally sharing with Turkish Cypriots the new republic's powers and responsibilities along with its economic benefits that now include EU membership. The latter will demand not just creating a new relationship across the Green Line, but also reaching out across the Mediterranean to Turkey,[199] where there is a perceived threat posed by a potentially hostile Cyprus.[200] This perception was exacerbated in the late 1990s when Greek Cypriots purchased ground-to-air missiles from Russia, which caused Turkey to respond with threats to destroy the missile sites and emphasize integration of the TRNC with mainland Turkey.[201] This would be accomplished by increasing the number of Turkish settlers, who had been moving to the island since 1974, in spite of UN condemnation of such a policy.[202] Turkish Cypriots are beyond where they were in the early days of the negotiations following the division. They are economically and politically stronger now than during earlier efforts to solve the problem. Perhaps they are waiting for some recognition from Islamic countries and

---

[198] *Ibid.* at 78. Basically, all for one side and none for the other.

[199] *Ibid. at 97*

[200] TRIANGLE OF CONFLICT – AND OPPORTUNITY, *supra* note 184, at 10.

[201] *Ibid.* at 6-7.

[202] *Ibid.* at Introduction.

links with EU members in order to improve their bargaining position. The bottom line is that each side will need to decide what its best alternative to a negotiated agreement (BATNA) will be. Unless both sides decide concurrently that "on balance" a negotiated agreement will be better than their respective default positions, once again there will be no settlement.[203]

So where does all this leave the problem that has divided Cyprus since the Turkish troops arrived in 1974, which has been discussed with almost daily regularity beyond that date, and now has languished without any definitive proposals from September 2008, when the current round of direct talks commenced intended to reach a final settlement? In this year, 2013, we are looking back 39 years to 1974 and 50 years to 1963 during which the passage of time has dictated its own version of history. Not the least of this is that the international community seems to have given up on the Cyprus Problem, leaving only what Rolandis describes as "the boring, tasteless and shallow reverberating voices of some politicians: 'We shall never sell out, we shall never yield.'" He charges that these are the same politicians who proclaim that "[i]n the new year, we shall celebrate." Notwithstanding these proclamations, there are those Greek Cypriots who feel that their "timid, foolish and spineless policies over the past years (despite the objections of some of us) have probably led to a total loss." Rolandis further asserts that there has been no "in-depth analysis" of the problem, only "sloganeering" without substance, relying on claims that those on each side are "victims of injustice" without acknowledging the commission of wrongs themselves.[204]

---

[203] Stavrinides, *supra* note 187, at 97-98.

[204] Nicos A. Rolandis, *After So Many "Nos", Shall we Whisper "Yes, We Can"?* CYPRUS MAIL, Jan. 11, 2009, http://www.cyprus-

143

The question that demands an answer is: Why, after all these years and so many efforts internally and internationally, is the problem still apparently irresolvable and intractable, leaving the parties without a negotiated agreement?

Cyprus: An Example of Traditional Spoiling

In her extensive study of the problem, Amira Schiff suggests that the history of unsuccessful negotiation of ethno-national conflicts demonstrates the need to analyze how *pre-negotiation* efforts can assist in achieving success in formal negotiations that follow.[205] In the case of the Cyprus negotiations, she says there is indication that the pre-negotiation process from 2003 to 2004 was deficient because its sole purpose was to enable the two respective leaders to benefit politically and was not based on the need to reach an agreement. Schiff feels they engaged in a pre-negotiation "game-theory" process that was cooperative but was followed by closed end negotiations. She points out that the Annan Plan did not provide the BATNA for either leader so there was no interest in making binding threats during the negotiations. Thus, she concludes the exercise became nothing more than a cooperative game that translated to one that became strictly non-cooperative, and failing to reach agreement only provided rewards that encouraged use of conflict strategies designed to maximize those payoffs. So the parties expressed a lack of flexibility, highlighted the lack of seriousness of the other negotiator, and emphasized the advantages of non-agreement over an agreement concerning the proposed plan. Therefore, Schiff

---

mail.com/news/main.php?id=43451&archive=1. Rolandis is a former foreign minister of the Republic of Cyprus.

[205] Amira Schiff, Prenegotiation [sic] and its Limits in Ethno-National Conflicts: A Systematic Analysis of Process and Outcomes in the Cyprus Negotiations, 13 INT'L NEG. 387, 388-408 (2008).

notes, early on both Denktash and Papadopoulos contributed to the negotiation failure. Each leader operated from the standpoint of protecting his status. For example, Denktash was more concerned about pressure exerted on him by Turkey than that coming from the international community. In the case of the Cyprus negotiations, her opinion is that it seems that both leaders felt secure in resorting to their initial positions in opposing the plan when they exhorted their respective constituencies to reject it at the polls in voting on the referendum in each community. Schiff finds it interesting to note that the two leaders came to the bargaining table as a result of pressure from outside third parties, even though believing that no agreement would be the best alternative to the Annan Plan.[206]

According to Schiff's research, the purpose of the pre-negotiation stage is to provide a transition that allows the parties to move from adversarial to collaborative perceptions and behaviors. In the case of Cyprus, the pre-negotiation approach regarding adoption of the Annan Plan was intended to begin the problem solving process uniting the opposing parties against the problem rather than themselves. Each was supposed to consider the interests and underlying needs of the other along with those of their own. Instead, the result was simply a means of managing the current circumstances. In her opinion, had the respective leaders been willing to change their beliefs and expectations, they might have been successful in considering collaborative options. They may have succeeded in electing "the option of conflict resolution through negotiation as an alternative to the unilateral track" that ultimately resulted in failure of efforts to resolve the decades-old divisive dispute.[207]

In analyzing how the two leaders could have been

---

[206] *Ibid.* at 388-408.

[207] *Ibid.*

145

successful, Schiff says that it is necessary to consider what factors would have contributed to de-escalation of the conflict, which would have required changes in their respective political positions, perceptions of the conflict, reasons for negotiating, and readiness to negotiate and implement any agreement reached. For example, historically, the UN, EU, US, and to some extent Greece and Turkey, have intervened as third parties and, along with Denktash and Papadopoulos, contributed in various ways to the failure of the process. Schiff acknowledges that, while there is no guarantee of success for even those pre-negotiations that proceed as planned, eventual positive results of the actual negotiations will depend on the foundation established and pursued during the pre-negotiation process, which is based on the following:[208]

- Jointly exploring the risks of reaching agreement.
- Assessing the costs of reaching agreement.
- Looking for alternatives to the problem.
- Setting an agenda for negotiations.
- Commitment to reciprocity in concessions.
- Seeking domestic support from both communities.
- Working toward perceptual changes from zero-sum to win-win.
- Careful and restrained intervention by outside third parties.

At one point in the recent past, then US Secretary of State Hillary Rodham Clinton announced that the Obama administration did "not plan to impose anything . . . [but] would like to support as far as we can the negotiations and we consider the best result to be a solution based on a two-

---

[208] *Ibid.*

146

zone and two-community federation."[209] Although the pre-negotiation process approach is helpful in working toward a positive platform to support a potentially satisfactory negotiation outcome, it nevertheless relies primarily on the intentions and actions of the *principal negotiators* and the involved *outside third party interveners.*

This is "one of the most complicated political cases, which the 20th century left us with."[210] As the Cyprus case clearly demonstrates, I feel there must be an additional element to provide the impetus to "close the deal" when necessary and create the most favorable climate for successful implementation following the reaching of an agreement. My work with Cypriots has convinced me that the *grassroots communities of civil society* on both sides of the division provide that additional critical element.

Absence of Civil Society: Negative Impact

There appears to have been "no serious attempt... [made to] empirically establish the relationship between the pre-negotiation stage and final negotiation results."[211] In the case of the Cyprus Problem, Zenon Stavrinides is of the opinion that the numerous failures over the years regarding the negotiations can only be classified as *pre in nature.* He says this has left members of both communities as "apathetic and cynical," causing them to "vote the way their preferred parties indicate in any new referendum."[212]

---

[209] *See U.S. Does Not Plan to Impose Solution to Cyprus Issue,* FOCUS INFORMATION AGENCY, Apr. 23, 2009, http://www.focus-fen.net (last visited May 5, 2009) (on file with author).

[210] *See* Maria Spassova, *Five Years After Rejecting the Annan's Plan, Cyprus is Still Searching for Solutions,* GR REPORTER, Apr. 23, 2009, http://www.grreporter.info/en/node/680.

[211] *See* Schiff, *supra* note 205, at 389.

[212] *See* Stavrinides, *supra* note 187.

147

To me, this is indicative of the need to bring the grassroots civil society into the process, something that has not been done to date.

In an effort to make it clear that the *status quo* in Cyprus was unacceptable and that both sides desired a federal solution seeking to design a new procedure to prepare the ground for substantive negotiations, Papadopoulos and Talat met with UN Under-Secretary-General Ibrahim Gambari on July 8, 2006, in Nicosia. Without reference to the Annan Plan, the two leaders agreed to create four technical committees that would deal with everyday matters, and several working groups that would discuss basic issues dealing with the Cyprus conflict. During the following months the discussions in the working groups and technical meetings concentrated on the political structure of the proposed new state and the efforts by Greek Cypriots to obtain agreement from Turkish Cypriots to cease building and development on Greek Cypriot-owned properties in the north, without any consideration for such a moratorium. The Turkish Cypriots refused. Thus, while Greek Cypriots may have thought they preserved much by voting against the referendum, actually they lost at least three major areas on the island to development and building activities of Turkish Cypriots, "circumstances which helped unleash what Greek Cypriot media call 'a building orgasm.'"[213]

Stavrinides says that it was never Talat's intention to permit the Gambari Agreement to replace the Annan Plan. On the other hand, Papadopoulos, notwithstanding charges that his "do-nothing policy" and his "poor diplomatic record" dealing with the Cyprus Problem resulted in "the cementing of the *de facto* partition of the island," sought to ignore the Plan. Papadopoulos intended the Gamabari Agreement to be the vehicle for preparation

---

[213] *Ibid. at 93-94.*

of the talks so that the Annan Plan would not come to the table again. So while Papadopoulos was attempting to obtain Talat's consent to abide by the Gambari Agreement and authorize Turkish Cypriot officials to immediately start work, Talat was expressing his interest in having officials initiate preliminary work as the preparation for subsequent substantive negotiations that would involve the two leaders on a schedule that could achieve final settlement by the end of the year (2008). Papadopoulos resisted any imposition of a time limit and insisted that negotiations between the two leaders could not start before the technical committees and working groups had completed their work in framing the issues that were the cause of the division.[214]

Stavrinides notes that today the Turkish Cypriots are stronger economically and politically than they have been during earlier efforts to reunify the island. He says the irony is that while Papadopoulos was banking on "Cyprus in the EU and Turkey knocking at the door," Talat and the Turkish leadership may have been contemplating a scenario whereby possible recognition of the TRNC by even a handful of Islamic governments with resulting links to EU states regarding direct trade and transport would cause the Greek Cypriots to capitulate to a settlement that would greatly reduce the amount of land to be returned to them.[215] Once again, it is a question of weighing the respective determination of each side as to what are their best alternatives to a negotiated agreement. Clearly apparent in this conflict over a divided island that could be reunited under terms and conditions that will improve the quality of life for all residents and stabilize this important area that is the crossroads from the Middle East to Europe, is the exclusion of *civil society* from the bargaining table. Perhaps these repeated failures will lead to the design of a pre-

---

[214] *Ibid. at 95-96*

[215] *Ibid. at 97-98*

negotiation process that will affect positively the formal negotiations that follow. Stavrinides feels that it only serves to perpetuate the failures of the past if we argue that:[216]

- The pre-negotiation process and subsequent formal negotiations are and should remain the province of the *political elite from the top down*, because they "reflect the wishes and needs" of most members of the respective communities.
- The community members would start negotiating where the two leaders have left off.
- "[T]he two leaders and the establishments in their communities have the political experience and realism to see they cannot get from negotiations what they would ideally like."
- A majority of the people on both sides "are apathetic and cynical by now" and "they will vote the way their preferred parties indicate in any new referendum."

Pre-Negotiation Must Precede Negotiations

After a history of colonialism followed by havoc and internal fighting inflamed by hatred resulting in civil war, arrival of foreign troops, displacement of thousands of people, loss of lives, destruction of entire families, and loss of land, it is time to search for a different approach to resolution of this conflict. It is time for a new look that can reach the attitudes and prejudices encompassed in the mutually utilized term, "The Other."[217] This means the exploration and consideration of attitudes, hatreds, prejudices, and demonizing that are reachable only at that

---

[216] *See* Stavrinides, *supra* note 187.

[217] *See generally* YIANNIS PAPADAKIS, ECHOES FROM THE DEAD ZONE: ACROSS THE CYPRUS DIVIDE (2005) (exploring the attitudes and prejudices that run deep in the Greek Cypriot world and seeking to discover "The Other" – the much maligned Turks).

level of *civil society* that permits resort to the commonality of the humanity of those locked in conflict.

According to Schiff, the potential of the pre-negotiation process was not fully achieved for several reasons. Among these was the failure to jointly explore the risks of agreement, understand the high cost of non-agreement, express belief in reciprocity, establish support from their respective communities, communicate the respective differences between the leaders defining the problems and necessary solutions, and create a genuine approach to reconciliation setting the stage for perceptual changes. Additionally, strong manipulation by the outside third parties such as the UN, EU, US, Greece and Turkey, failed to accomplish entirely the critical functions of effective pre-negotiation.[218] As predicted, the efforts of the political elite have failed.[219] Javier Perez de Cuellar served as the Secretary-General of the UN from 1982-1991, and he is of the firm belief that the Cyprus Problem is not "easily susceptible to a reasonable solution." He minces no words when he says, " After my own sustained effort of more than 12 years, I would characterize the Cyprus problem as a maze in which each promising pathway leads back to the starting point."[220]

Christofias and Talat, began meeting in September 2008 and, although not successful, there appears to have been some expression of optimism from each as to a possible final settlement by autumn 2009.[221] Christofias has

---

[218] *See* Schiff, *supra* note 205, at 400-406.

[219] JAVIER PÉREZ DE CUÉLLAR, PILGRIMAGE FOR PEACE: A SECRETARY-GENERAL'S MEMOIR 25 (1997) ("[S]omething more than perfection was required to bring agreement between the Greek and Turkish communities . . . .").

[220] *Ibid.*

[221] Stefanos Evripidou, *Christofias More Optimistic After Talks than Before*, CYPRUS MAIL, Feb. 13, 2009, http://www.cyprus-

151

been accused of abandoning the Annan Plan "and renegotiating the entire settlement from scratch, [making] it . . . obvious that he would enter [into] an interminable and unproductive procedure that would not lead to a deal even in 10 years."[222] Christofias has charged that the Turkish Cypriots are really looking for a confederation rather than a federation by attempting to weaken the proposed federal government's role and functions.[223] Not to be outdone, the Turkish Cypriots claim that Greek Cypriots are defaming the Turkish Cypriots position in the negotiations.[224]

Since the Greek Cypriots rejected "the only comprehensive settlement plan prepared by the UN in the last [41] years"[225] despite prior acceptance by Turkish Cypriots, other avenues need to be explored to move the conflict to a level where it can be resolved, if still possible. Otherwise, the extensive history of spoiling will likely repeat itself once again. "For several decades, the UN has continuously worked to persuade the *two communities* to find a viable solution to the Cyprus issue,"[226] but the so-called peace process continues just as it has for several decades, without any positive results. One yet to be tried approach may be the only alternative remaining with potential for providing a solution: Facilitation of *civil society* discourse through grassroots efforts by citizens on either side of the Green Line.

mail.com/news/main.php?id=44010&cat_id=1.

[222] Loucas Charalambous, *President's Handling of Talks Hardly Inspires Confidence*, CYPRUS MAIL, Jan. 18, 2009, http://www.cyprus-mail.com/news/main.php?id=43585&cat_id=1.

[223] Mu Xuequan, *Rival Cypriot Communities Accuse Each Other for Lack of Progress on Reunification Talks*, CHINA VIEW, Jan. 14, 2009, http://news.xinhuanet.com/english/2009-01/14/content_10653309.htm

[224] *Ibid.*

[225] *See* Charalambous, *supra* note 222.

[226] *See* Xuequan, *supra* note 223 (emphasis added).

In order to achieve this it is necessary to look to the human condition and not the political realities. Rolandis argues that Cypriots need to feel they are "Cypriots first, and then Greeks or Turks." In doing so, he says they must rise above their history that is imbued with Greek Cypriot efforts to achieve enosis on the one hand, or partition (perhaps even island-wide occupation by Turkey) as the Turkish Cypriot dream on the other. Meanwhile, he feels that the international players have removed themselves from the conflict between both communities. On the one hand, he notes that the Greek Cypriot Republic of Cyprus was recognized formally. On the other, he points out that the international players endorsed "pragmatic positions" that "are not palatable to many Cypriots." The current peace talks in Cyprus take place under what he calls an "unstable atmosphere" because it appears that the following are the main subjects of negotiation: (1) Method of electing the president and vice president on a single ballot to be used to cast votes throughout the entire island, (2) the continuing presence of Turkish troops posing the threat of military intervention by Turkey, and (3) the difficult question of property rights.[227] Failure to achieve a settlement most likely will result in partition.[228] The present "relatively tranquil status quo" is not something capable of indefinite preservation.[229] There is even talk of a

---

[227] *See* Nicos A. Rolandis, *The Beautiful People, Enosis, Partition . . . and Our Bloody Mess*, CYPRUS MAIL, Feb. 15, 2009, http://www.cyprus-mail.com/news/main.php?id=44065&archive=1 [hereinafter *The Beautiful People*].

[228] *See* International Crisis Group, *Cyprus: Reversing the Drift to Partition* 1, EUROPE REPORT NO. 190, Jan. 10, 2008, http://www.crisisgroup.org/home/index.cfm?id=5945&1=1 (last visited June 9, 2009).

[229] *Ibid.*

153

"Taiwanisation" process[230] that will accelerate and consolidate.[231] Greek Cypriots, Turkish Cypriots, and Turkey all will suffer if this comes to pass.[232] Renewal of stressful relations between the EU and NATO, long years of EU and Turkey friction, increased division between Christians and Muslims, and the possibility of new military tensions arising on the southeastern edge of the EU will also be the price paid for failure to reunify the island.[233]

According to the ancient Greek playwright Aeschylus, listening "to one of two sides, [one] learns only half the truth."[234] The two respective current leaders must therefore "listen carefully to each other and seek justice after taking into account the arguments, the mistakes, the omissions and the sins of all Cypriots. Otherwise, Cyprus will remain divided into two parts, which does not serve the interests of either the Greek or the Turkish Cypriots."[235] Both sides will benefit by another effort at reunification that will take place sooner than later.[236] Because of the length of time already lost, the Greek Cypriots should move

---

[230] *Ibid.* at 25-26. Turkish Cypriots could begin to see their part of the island as their homeland and will be committed to express loyalty to it. This will emphasize the importance of a separate Turkish Cypriot culture rather than including Turkish Cypriots solely as part of the Greek Cypriot Republic of Cyprus, not unlike the movement for a separate Taiwanese culture separate from China.

[231] *Ibid.*

[232] *Ibid.*

[233] *See* Hugh Pope, *Cyprus: "Things are Looking Up"*, INTERNATIONAL CRISIS GROUP, Sep. 17, 2008, http://www.crisisgroup.org/home/index.cfm?id=5731&1=1 (last visited June 9, 2009).

[234] *The Beautiful People, supra* note 227.

[235] *Ibid.*

[236] JAMES KER-LINDSAY, EU ACCESSION AND UN PEACEMAKING IN CYPRUS 136 (2005).

154

quickly.[237] With every passing year the argument becomes stronger for those who question whether forcing "two people who have lived apart for so long to cohabit closely is really a viable option."[238] This view only becomes stronger as reunification continues to be delayed.[239] As it is, the prediction that Greek Cypriot rejection of the Annan Plan in 2004 would make any following effort much less favorable to them seems likely to be the reality.[240] Recent polling disclosed that five years after the divided referendum results, most of the Turkish Cypriot community would now reject the Annan Plan if given a chance to vote again.[241]

Accomplishment of what Rolandis has urged (to consider "the arguments, the mistakes, the omissions and the sins of all Cypriots"[242]), it is necessary that Cypriot *civil society* on both sides of the Green Line be able to express their interests and underlying needs at the bargaining table.[243] Active community participation will help ensure the success of the negotiation process and subsequent

---

[237] *Ibid.*

[238] *Ibid.*

[239] *Ibid.*

[240] *Ibid.*

[241] *See Today Most of Turkish Cypriots Would Reject Annan Plan: Poll*, FOCUS INFORMATION AGENCY, Mar. 5, 2009, http://www.focus-fen.net (last visited March 5, 2009) (on file with author). Results among 1,387 residents of Northern Cyprus: 53.8% against, 27.9% favorable, 3.15% don't know, and 15.1% undecided.

[242] *The Beautiful People, supra* note 227.

[243] *See generally* Anthony Wanis-St. John & Darren Kew, *Civil Society and Peace Negotiations: Confronting Exclusion*, 13 INT'L NEG. 11 (2008) (finding, upon survey of a wide variety of different peace processes, a strong correlation between active civil society participation in peace negotiations and the durability of peace during the peace building phase).

155

efforts to implement any agreement.[244] But even this is not enough. The people on the ground on either side must first *listen to* and fully *hear* each other in order to put themselves in the shoes of those they face and understand what they are feeling from another point of view. This is the process of *humanization* that reverses the negative effect of *demonization* and enables parties in conflict to empathize with each other without blaming or judging.

Kenneth Cloke defines demonization as a destructive process by which "we define our enemies" through accusations of evil, the ultimate purpose of which is "to create the *self*-permission, win the approval of outsiders, and establish the moral logic required to justify committing evil oneself," using the following principal elements:[245]

- The other side intended to cause us harm.
- All ideas or statements made by the other side are either wrong or submitted for dishonest purposes.
- Everything negative is the fault of the other side.
- The other side wants to destroy our values and us so we need to destroy them first.
- Benefits to the other side will harm us, and harm to them will benefit us.
- Criticism of us or praise for the other side is an act of disloyalty and treason.
- Without exception, all on the other side are enemies.
- If you are not with us you are against us.

---

[244] *Ibid.* at 33.

[245] *See* KENNETH CLOKE, CONFLICT REVOLUTION: MEDIATING EVIL, WAR, INJUSTICE AND TERRORISM: HOW MEDIATORS CAN HELP SAVE THE PLANET 173, 179-183 (2008).

- We have nothing in common with the other side and it is dangerous to consider them human.
- It is impossible to conduct dialogue with the other side or negotiate or cooperate with them to resolve the conflicts we have with them.
- The evil represented by the other side gives us permission to act with hostility toward them, just as they feel and act toward us.

Dismantling the wall erected by demonization presents a difficult challenge. This is especially true concerning the Cyprus Problem that has existed for so long in a perpetual and self-energizing manner. It is possible, however, to deconstruct and transform the elements of demonization through the use of mediation. An important part of this is the "need to recognize the ways that attribution of evil are subtly reflected in the language and syntax we use to describe our conflicts, enemies, issues, and selves."[246] It will be necessary to create a balance "between looking back to 'neutralize history' and looking forward to build a new society."[247] The current thinking is that both looking back and looking forward are necessary. Without intensely looking at the atrocities of the past there is not much hope of achieving a transformation.

There will be more future problems if there is a failure to examine past crimes. How this is accomplished will depend on local demand and local culture. This process is not the same as forgetting the past; rather it is the ability to separate one from the other, and let go of what has already gone by in favor of seeking closure in order to

---

[246] *Ibid.*

[247] STEPHEN RYAN, THE TRANSFORMATION OF VIOLENT INTERCOMMUNAL CONFLICT 159, 159-160 (2007).

move on. An important consideration is that the structural changes any two leaders are attempting may not succeed in achieving transformative change if these efforts fail to convince the respective citizenry to forgive for their *own* sake, and address the specific needs of the very people living in the communities under siege.[248] So it seems the customary consideration of truth and then reconciliation in that order would best be *reversed,* since it is only after reconciliation has been commenced that the truth can surface.[249]

Because one side's attempt to do justice on their own terms in the aftermath of conflict will be viewed by the other side as a way of continuing or resuming the war by what is claimed to be fair only in the eyes of the winners, the preferable approach is to use power politics and search for an accommodation that is mutually acceptable, ignore the past, and move on to build a peaceful future. If the parties are to work to avoid repeating the past, however, an agreement must be reached regarding the nature of the wrongs committed and how the future will be different. A rational consensus needs to be built concerning a description of the past so that a reasonable agreement can be reached regarding the dreadful acts that were perpetrated on both sides. The goal should be the construction of a consensus about contested history as to real victims and real oppressors in order to reach a just way to bury the past. Since prosecution of human rights violations could jeopardize peace in the aftermath of civil conflict, prudence dictates that the political process permit constraints on the retributive portion of the effort, so that offenders as well as

---

[248] *Ibid.*

[249] Nigel Biggar, *Conclusion, in* BURYING THE PAST: MAKING PEACE AND DOING JUSTICE AFTER CIVIL CONFLICT 309, 309-313 (Nigel Biggar ed., 2003).

victims have a stake in a future where their respective rights will be considered.[250]

Ironically, Jay Rothman has noted that the negotiation process can worsen a conflict so, while pre-negotiation is essential to prepare the grassroots for the formal negotiations, an effective *confidence-building* approach is a necessity. Rothman points to this as being emphasized by U.S. secretary of state James Baker when referring to the 1991 Middle East Peace Conference as a failure "to deal adequately with the human dimension of the conflict" by all parties, which is a necessity in supporting the negotiation process that must "send signals of peace and reconciliation that affect the people of the region."[251] To accomplish this, the antagonism, resonance, invention, and action (ARIA) approach, advanced by Rothman was designed and applied in the historical conflict between the Israelis and the Palestinians.[252] This is the process in brief:

- *Antagonism* is dealt with by asking the parties to express their respective views of the problem, state how they view the other side in terms of the issue, describe what limited resources are at stake, and summarize their respective positions on the outcomes they would like to achieve in

[250] *Ibid.*

[251] JAY ROTHMAN, RESOLVING IDENTITY-BASED CONFLICT IN NATIONS, ORGANIZATIONS, AND COMMUNITIES 87, 87-167(1997). Jay Rothman was the director of the Jerusalem Peace Initiative from 1992-1994. Sponsored by the Leonard Davis Institute for International Relations at the Hebrew University of Jerusalem, the Jerusalem Peace Initiative conducted conflict resolution, dialogue, and training workshops between Israelis and Palestinians for various student, community, and political groups.

[252] *Ibid.*

future negotiations.

- *Resonance* is the surfacing of the human dimension existing underneath the antagonistic positions of each through providing the groundwork for understanding, expressing interactive introspection, and meshing the respective needs of the parties.
- *Invention* consists of brainstorming various possible approaches to a solution through the establishment of a statement of principles to be used related to five functional areas of mutual concern: security, economics, education, municipal services and governance, and cultural expression.
- *Action* deals with the consideration of the results of the work product of the mixed teams that suggest definite confidence-building initiatives to deal with the five policy proposals set forth under *Invention,* directed to project planning, institution building, and negotiation.

In order to successfully apply the ARIA approach, it is necessary that the parties in conflict be willing to transform their fighting and antagonism into "constructive engagement and resonance."[253] This can be achieved through the concept of a "Just Peace" that is "a process whereby peace and justice are reached together by two or more parties recognizing each other's identities, each renouncing some central demands, and each accepting to abide by common rules jointly developed," as language-oriented, and anticipates:[254]

---

[253] *Ibid.* at 167.
[254] *See* Pierre Allan & Alexis Keller, *The Concept of a Just Peace, or Achieving Peace Through Recognition, Renouncement, and Rule, in*

- Negotiators jointly building "a new common language" that redefines certain elements of their identity.
- Employment of a "bottom-up" approach that proposes "an accommodation process whereby negotiators seek to agree to a fair and lasting peace by crafting it in a manner deemed just by *all relevant protagonists.*"

Peace so achieved is just because three elements fall into place.[255]

- It is the result of an evolving recognition by the negotiators that there is a "series of conventions."
- It is expressed in a shared language that is sensitively respectful of all parties.
- It "does not reflect a blinkered vision of law."

According to this approach, four generally accepted principles are required to negotiate a peace that will be perceived as just and legitimate.[256]

- Thin recognition.
- Thick recognition.
- Renouncement.
- Common rule.

Adjustment to the prevailing circumstances is necessary. The four principles or conventions are not a list of requirements, but rather a process for both the preconditions to a Just Peace and the steps that will make it possible. [257]

WHAT IS A JUST PEACE? 195, 195-215 (Pierre Allan & Alexis Keller, eds. 2006).

[255] *Ibid.* at 196.

[256] *Ibid.* at 197.

[257] *Ibid.* at 197-209.

161

- As the first convention, *Thin Recognition* refers to the fact that each party accepts the other as a human being.
- As the second convention, *Thick Recognition* refers to the fact that each party understands the fundamental features of the other party's identity.
- As the third convention, *Renouncement* refers to the fact that concessions and compromise are required to create a Just Peace.
- As the fourth convention, *Rule* refers to the fact that a Just Peace must not be entirely subjective, but rather out in the open within the view of the public with explicit, legitimate, and objective rules for settlement, acceptable behavior, and yardsticks so that all may approve of any proposed solution.

The concept of a Just Peace requires that each party understand and accept the fundamental identity of the other party, especially those differences in features that it requires to maintain its "self," so that there can be a "reaching out" of a universal formula lumping all parties together. The central feature of our world is that there are many identities that demand recognition, and they all need to be respected and honored.[258]

John Paul Lederach coined the term *conflict transformation* in the 1980s. This was an outgrowth of his belief that conflict is normal between humans and that "constructive change efforts... include, and go beyond, the resolution of specific problems." The goal is "the building of healthy relationships and communities, locally and globally. It requires real change in our current ways of

---

[258] *Ibid.* at 215.

relating."[259] Thus, if we are to examine the Cyprus Problem in terms of management or resolution, we are looking at change per se. Perhaps that is what has been the difficulty with use of the word *resolution* of the *problem* on both sides of the Green Line. Since nothing else has worked over the close to half a century during which this difficult situation has presented itself to the international community, a new approach is necessary. The parties must *transform* the conflict, rather than continue to trudge in the morass of efforts to manage or resolve it. Irrespective of whether their feeling is that a continued elite top-down approach is appropriate, or that a bottom-up change should be encouraged, the emphasis needs to shift dramatically from the two leaders who are working the floor as if the dispute were theirs alone. The inescapable conclusion is that such a shift must involve members on the ground in both communities so that they can learn and practice the interactive human approach emphasized by a transformation of their conflict.

Paula M. Pickering has observed the problem in connection with peacebuilding efforts in the Balkans.[260] She points out that a multilevel network model of peacebuilding needs to be applied to ongoing peace projects in societies that are deeply divided. Her analysis encourages an understanding of problems created by "putative homeland elites," agendas of national and local-level minority activists, and proffered assistance to civil society coming from Western concepts instead of understanding of local mechanisms grounded in a

---

[259] JOHN PAUL LEDERACH, THE LITTLE BOOK OF CONFLICT TRANSFORMATION 3, 4-5 (2003).

[260] *See* PAULA M. PICKERING, PEACEBUILDING IN THE BALKANS: THE VIEW FROM THE GROUND FLOOR 187, 187-188 (2007).

recovering society.[261] Pickering emphasizes that paying attention to views of the grassroots elements concerning peacebuilding reveals the weakness of post-conflict institutions in recovering communities. Key considerations in her astute analysis caution that dismissal of "the enduring informal mechanisms that ordinary people use to help address the everyday aspects of reconstruction in favor of top-down formal institutions may well be a serious impediment to peacebuilding efforts in the region...[and the] importance of listening to and observing ordinary people struggling to cope in postwar societies cannot be overstated."[262] Although the preceding was written with respect to peacebuilding efforts in the Balkans, it similarly serves as a reflection of the 50-year history of attempts to bring peace to and reunify the island of Cyprus.

The much-celebrated Talat-Christofias talks were deadlocked notwithstanding attempts to camouflage that fact, "hoping, against all hope, that some miracle [could] still come their way." Instead, acrimony and anger replaced the cordiality that existed when those talks began. For instance, Talat was accused of being the "uncompromising partitionist leader" that Denktash personified. Also, Talat "accused Christofias of negotiating in bad faith, making international agreements presuming that the existing Greek Cypriot Republic will live forever." When Christofias, and Talat, started their talks in 2008, the atmosphere indicated that this was "the last real chance of peace and reconciliation in Cyprus." Christofis has, however, effectively rejected the key provisions of the Annan Plan regarding the property issues. Furthermore, "the support is minimal at the [Greek Cypriot] grass roots for a genuinely equal power sharing with the Turkish Cypriots in a new State on the island." Most Greek Cypriots "do not want to

---

[261] *Ibid.* at 187-188.

[262] *Ibid.*

164

give up the existing Greek Cypriot Republic of Cyprus, now an EU member for any new State in partnership with the Turkish Cypriots."[263]

In recent years, the 35-year ban by Britain's Civilian Aviation Authority concerning direct flights between UK airports and Northern Cyprus was challenged in the Administrative Court (a division of the UK High Court). A decision in favor of the airline challenger would effectively end the isolation of the Turkish Cypriot community. The challenge was traceable to former UK Prime Minister Tony Blair's comments in May 2004. When visiting Turkey, he commented on the isolation and inconvenience created by the ban on direct flights to and from the northern part of the island: "I think it is important . . . that we end the isolation of Northern Cyprus . . . . That means lifting the embargoes in respect to trade, and in respect to air travel."[264] In July 2009, however, the challenge was defeated in the UK court and the request for review of the current ban was dismissed.[265]

As of October 17, 2004, new construction was booming in the northern part of the island and Greek Cypriot land sales there were "worth more than two billion dollars."[266] However, the top court of the EU recently

[263] Ozay Mehmet, *Guest Comment: The End of the Cyprus Problem*, FinancialMirror.com, Feb. 19, 2009, http://www.financialmirror.com/Columnist/COMMENT/262.

[264] *See* Max de Trense, *Challenge to Ban on Direct Flights to Northern Cyprus Will Be Heard in High Court*, SYS-CON Media, Inc., Apr. 17, 2009, http://www.sys-con.com/node/924037.

[265] *See UK Court Says No to Direct Flights to the North*, CYPRUS MAIL, July 29, 2009, http://www.cyprus-mail.com/news/main.php?id=47057&cat_id=1.

[266] *See* Philippos Savvides, *Written Evidence Submitted by Dr. Philippos Savvides, Research Fellow, Hellenic Foundation for European and Foreign Policy (ELIAMEP)*, Oct. 17, 2004, *available at* http://www.publications.parliament.uk/pa/cm200405/cmselect/cmfaff/113/4101901.htm (follow "Written evidence submitted

rendered a turning point decision that allows Greek Cypriot courts to assert jurisdiction over these issues favoring Greek Cypriot claims to ownership of their land in the North.[267] Exacerbating the problem are two key facts. First, the EU may punish Turkey for declining to open its ports to Greek Cypriot shipping and refusing to acknowledge the legitimacy of the Greek Cypriot government. Second, Turkish Cypriots are becoming "Turkified" because an increasing number of people emigrated from Turkey since 1994, placing more of the north under Turkey's dominance. The course and progression of the Christofias-Talat talks seemed to remove any incentive for either side to negotiate. They appeared to "simply vanish. No one will walk away from the talks having accomplished anything. Instead, any peacemaking attempts will melt away like spring snow. And with that, the last hope for a united Cyprus will also disappear."[268]

That prophesy seems to have come true. Talat's authority was "shaken" following the right-wing National Unity Party victories over his Republican Turkish Party in the April 2009, Northern Cyprus parliamentary elections.[269] This subsequently resulted in the center-left Talat being replaced by Eroglu in the negotiations, notwithstanding statements by both the Turkish president and prime minister that Talat was "the only negotiator" for them."[270]

---

by Dr. Philippos Savvides" hyperlink).

[267] See Helena Smith, *Scent of Victory Among Lemon Trees as Displaced Cypriots Win Claim on Ancestral Land: Displaced Greek Cypriots Celebrate Landmark Court Ruling on Property Rights*, GUARDIAN.CO.UK, May 1, 2009, http://www.guardian.co.uk/world/2009/may/01/cyprus-displaced-european-union-greece.

[268] *Ibid.*

[269] See Spassova, *supra note210.*

[270] *Ibid.*

166

Supporters of reunification hoping that Talat's role as negotiator would continue to be supported by the large number of voters in the north who seek an agreement that provides EU membership were sadly disappointed by the result of the 2010 election of a new Turkish Cypriot leader.[271] Adding to this is the difficult issue of "return or compensation of properties in the north owned by Greek Cypriots displaced to the south."[272] The concern is that the managing coalition of the Greek Cypriot republic's government is in danger of falling apart because of criticism from Nikolas Papadopoulos, deputy chairman of the Democratic Party and son of the late president Tassos Papadopoulos, over the policies of Christofias (who was Talat's political ally before the 1974 division) regarding the Cyprus Problem and his alleged concessions to Talat.[273]

Now is Time for All Cypriots to Take Charge

The last best hope for reunification of the island of Cyprus rests in the hands of the people at the grassroots level on both sides. They must understand their actual empowerment to change the game through conflict transformation from the bottom-up. This is their BATNA given the current state of the stalled negotiation process. The goals that must be pursued are personal, relational, structural, and cultural.[274] The grassroots communities need

---

[271] *See* Sven G. Simonsen, *Cyprus: Are Old Friends Offering New Hope For Unity?* CHRISTIAN SCIENCE MONITOR, May 6, 2009, http://www.csmonitor.com/2009/0507/p06s01-woeu.html.
[272] *Ibid.*

[273] *Ibid. See also Will the Governing Coalition in Cyprus Collapse?* GR REPORTER, Apr. 13, 2009, http://www.grreporter.info/en/node/645.

[274] *See* Lederach, *supra* note 259, at 27.

167

to develop their respective capacities to cultivate personal practices that will:[275]

- Present divisive issues as a window of opportunity.
- Integrate the various time frames, present as well as future.
- Change the energies of conflict from an "either/or" emphasis to one of "both/and frame of reference."
- Convert complexity from an enemy to a collaborator.
- Understand and respect the role of identity.

Such an endeavor is something new to the efforts to deal with the conflict because it requires a decided shift from an *adversarial* to a *collaborative* game. While this endeavor provides much hope for success, it also faces a rough road to travel due to the historical and traditional rut that has consumed efforts to solve the Cyprus Problem. Many reasons contribute to the extreme difficulty of the conflict, including the simple fact that Turkish Cypriots live on 37 percent of the island, but constitute only one-fifth of the island's population.[276] They fear that a mandated property return under an Annan Plan type of settlement would seal their minority social status through a smaller area allocated to their community, and degrade economic opportunities because of their inability to provide compensation to Greek Cypriot owners for the land that would not be returned.[277] Adding to this difficulty is deep

---

[275] *Ibid.* at 48-60.

[276] *See* Simonsen, *supra* note 271.

[277] *Ibid.* Returning Greek Cypriot owned land would further reduce Turkish Cypriot territory, while retaining the land would not be possible because of Turkish Cypriot financial inability to compensate the Greek Cypriot owners.

division over the system of government following reunification. Turkish Cypriot insistence on *minority* rights is pitted against Greek Cypriot emphasis on *individual* rights, and the dilemma posed by "citizenship rights for tens of thousands of settlers from Turkey."[278] Greek Cypriots seek a future that resembles the past, "a Greek-Cypriot-dominated virtually unitary Cyprus," and the Turkish Cypriots want one that "resembles, as far as possible, the *de facto* two-state present."[279] This impasse is a result of the development of a dual personality for the island known as "Dementia Cypria."[280] As is the case with the human condition of dual personalities, the challenge becomes one of reconciling the two so that neither dominates the other.

The ineffective manner of interaction that has been the model for close to half a century is all too easy to accept. The challenge that faces those who truly desire a reunification is the bravery required to change course through education, training, and adoption of the ARIA approach and to seek a Just Peace. Emphasis needs to be redirected away from the contest over the island's "factual" history, and instead channeled towards memories that deal effectively with the past through present feelings in the everyday lives of ordinary Cypriots on both sides of the Green Line as they struggle with the issues that continue to divide them. People in both communities need to understand that the history of the conflict cannot be undone. They must focus instead on sharing their memories, because those are psychological expressions

---

[278] *Ibid.*

[279] *See* Zenon Stavrinides, *Dementia Cypria: On the Social Psychological Environment of the Intercommunal Negotiations*, 21 CYPRUS REV. 175, 175-186 (2009) [hereinafter *Dementia Cypria*].

[280] *Ibid.*

169

emanating from within themselves.[281] Given the current atmosphere on the island in both communities, the dwindling support from international outsiders, and the security issue present for both Greek and Turkish Cypriots because of the continued presence of Turkish troops in the North supporting a TRNC government for which Turkey pays "at least a third,"[282] the future admittedly does not look bright.

Throughout the lengthy history of the conflict the respective leaders of the Greek and Turkish Cypriot communities have consistently advocated separate sets of "political and ethical beliefs and desires – rational and irrational" that are "fundamentally incompatible."[283] So how can the current leaders who carry the baggage of their respective predecessors suddenly change course and ask their followers to throw off their historical shackles in order to join together for peace? How "can the two leaders ever acknowledge (the true history) to their own people and tell them that *they do not deserve* to get all they are demanding, as the other side also has just grievances and must secure their rights and protection?"[284] Even assuming those possibilities, how could these leaders "retain their authority with their respective communities if they sought sanity in a world of collective *dementia*?"[285] Political survival teaches otherwise.

It has been over five years since Christofias and Talat commenced their direct interaction to solve the Cyprus Problem that remains the only armed conflict in the

---

[281] *See* RACHEL M. MACNAIR , THE PSYCHOLOGY OF PEACE: AN INTRODUCTION 123, 123-125 (2003).

[282] *See* Simonsen, *supra* note 271.

[283] *See Dementia Cypria, supra* note 279.

[284] *Ibid.*

[285] *Ibid.*

EU. The conflict could continue to be an obstacle to Turkey's EU accession and to cooperation between NATO and the EU if Turkey cannot perform the role of "regional peacemaker/peacekeeper" while it acts as "a conduit for communications" with the expanded Middle East and joins its growing economy with that of Europe. There is a problem regarding how to ensure that each community will be a full federal participant. Apparently the process has come down to who will blink first. While some commentators feel that the process so far has been "unfruitful," others insist that much has been accomplished. Some suggest that the real decision makers have been Christofias and Turkish Prime Minister Recep Tayyip Erdogan (*not* Talat and *not* Eroglu), which makes a solution more difficult because Turkey has more to lose than gain from conceding on key points. The situation has been exacerbated further by the struggle between the Islamists and the secularists in Turkey, and the fact that Talat had to face re-election in 2010. Talat's questionable chances for re-election presented a serious dilemma for the Greek Cypriots who were waiting for the other side to concede. Delaying action until after the Turkish Cypriot 2010 elections could result in Talat failing to be re-elected and a hard-liner succeeding him, which is exactly what occurred. This was not unexpected because it was difficult to see how Talat could win in the absence of a solution.[286]

Even assuming that a solution can be achieved, what will be the result of the referenda that must follow any such agreement between the negotiators for the two sides? The polls have shown that what Turkish Cypriots may decide is no longer predictable because they are much less positive than they were at the time of the 2004 referenda.

---

[286] *See* Stefanos Evripidou, *The Talks: One Year On*, CYPRUS MAIL, Aug. 30, 2009, http://www.cyprus-mail.com/news/main.php?id=47548&_id=1 (last visited Sept. 20, 2009).

The elephant in the room is "the global economic crisis." In the event of a negative economic impact on Cyprus that "coincides with substantial movement in the talks," potential prosperity for the island through reunification might be just the thing necessary to surmount the historical obstacles that so far have prevented a solution. However, the UN has estimated that "9 out of 10 people on both sides still have no contact with persons from the other community." So the critical element for reunification will be the degree of willingness and determination of Cypriots to reject the ineffective rote motions of so-called "technical committees and working groups," and instead commit to becoming educated in the process of *humanization.* Greek and Turkish Cypriots alike must possess the strength to rise up and take destiny into their own hands while simultaneously dealing with difficult economic conditions in both communities.[287]

In this connection, a new effort has been presented by "ENGAGE," a fresh bi-communal grassroots attempt to encourage involvement of *civil society* on both sides to achieve reunification and peace "despite and against the wishes of incumbent political leadership." This would enable *civil society* to "effectively bypass obstacles politicians found hard to get around."[288] However, even this possibility could be doomed to fail if the estimate proves accurate that in addition to "steadily leaving" the island or moving to the Greek Cypriot south, Turkish Cypriots already may be outnumbered when compared to the immigrant population from Turkey.[289]These are

---

[287] *Ibid.*

[288] *See* Simon Bahceli, *Peace is Too Important to be Left to Politicians,* CYPRUS MAIL, April 2009, http://www.cyprus-mail.com/news/main.php?id=46669&_id=1 (last visited July 7, 2009).

[289] *See* Hugh Pope, *Waiting for Miracles on Cyprus,* CURRENT HISTORY (International Crisis Group), March 15, 2010, http://www.crisisgroup.org/home/index.cfm?id=6582&1=1 (last visited March 19, 2010).

extraordinary times for ordinary people who truly have the opportunity to take charge of their future. The question is whether they will seize the moment before it is too late.

EPILOGUE

The impotent struggle at the Track I level to achieve a peaceful long-term solution to the Cyprus Problem has seen the incessant deterioration of the best chance for settlement presented during the history of the conflict, namely the UN Annan Plan (version V) in 2004. This result has taken its heaviest toll on the Greek Cypriots who continually lose ground from what they would have received under that solution had they not voted against the 2004 referendum. It seems the longer the series of "negotiations" go nowhere the less the Greek Cypriots appear to be able to salvage under any settlement patterned after the failed Plan. One of the best examples is the incursion into the north of international investors who are seeking to capitalize on property values notwithstanding that those purchases generally consist of Greek Cypriot owned property and violate the historical international embargo that prohibits dealing with the Turkish Cypriots until a satisfactory solution to reunification has been reached, something the Greek Cypriots have steadfastly opposed since the 1974 division of the island. [290]

It seems that former Republic of Cyprus President Demetris Christofias had been criticized in his own community for being responsible for playing politics and creating a labyrinth making it impossible to extricate the apparently doomed peace talks. In turn, Christofias complained that the positions submitted by Turkish Cypriot leader Dervis Eroglu were more unfavorable than what Greek Cypriots would have received under the Annan Plan.

---

[290] *See* Anny Tzotzadini, *Northern Cyprus plans to become Mediterranean "Las Vegas,"* GREEK Europe REPORTER, July 21, 2010, http://eu.greekreporter-con/2010/07/21/northern-cyprus-plans-to-become-mediterranean-las-vegas (last visited Oct. 9, 2010).

Critics of Christofias advanced the argument that had he not worked to defeat the Annan Plan in the first place he would not have received proposals that were worse because he would have been talking about the *Plan* rather than alternatives. Seeking a better deal than what Eroglu was offering had put the Greek Cypriots in the unenviable position of trying to resurrect the lost opportunity of 2004, while at the same time having to respond to lesser terms. The reported conclusion was that, instead of seeking a settlement using the Annan Plan as the basis and moving forward without recriminations concerning demons of the past, Christofias commenced re-negotiating the conflict from the beginning when he was aware that without a settlement then Turkish Cypriot peace-oriented leader Mehmet Ali Talat's days in power were limited to only two remaining years. So what choice was left to the Greek Cypriots except agreeing to a partition? All the while lurking in the background was the fact that many Greek Cypriots, while not favorably disposed to the Annan Plan in its entirety as presented in 2004, had advocated approval with the idea of subsequently negotiating modifications.

Eroglu labeled the recent efforts between the two leaders as the last chance to achieve a settlement. Some felt that Talat, in losing the election to Eroglu, appeared to have been punished by the Turkish Cypriot electorate for failing to achieve peace during his term. However, it seems on the contrary that Eroglu may have defeated Talat because of an impression that Eroglu would not pursue peace talks but instead attempt to realize the long-sought-after Turkish Cypriot dream of securing recognition of what they refer to as their "Turkish Republic of Northern Cyprus" (TRNC), as an independent and sovereign state under Turkey's protection. One of the key elements here was the fact that Eroglu asserted there is no "right of return" for refugees because there is no longer any such category on the island. So, while he would concede to a limited number of Greek Cypriots returning to the northern part, Eroglu was against a full right of return, opting instead for exchange of property or financial compensation for loss. This is not what Christofias and his electorate envisioned as their solution.[291]

Over more than a half century of the conflict there has been a failure on both sides to deal with meaningful specifics. Instead there has been a continual barrage of emotional appeals employing "trigger" words and scare tactics censoring anyone who seeks to propose solutions to issues dealing with property, settlers (immigrants from Turkey), how each side is to be governed, missing persons, and creation of a new political structure on the island. These emotional appeals have enabled the "spoiling" process to survive so that nothing changes except the names of the respective political leaders of the two communities as they continue to wield power on the playing field, enabled by the absence of opposition from their respective constituents who remain in the bleachers through acceptance of their assumed role of "bystanders."

Historically, intractable conflicts generally are those where high emotions make separating the people from the problem to focus on interests rather than positions for mutual gain, almost impossible. This is especially true in the case of the Cyprus Problem. The alternative is to *transform* the conflict while disagreement continues. Achieving this transition requires the withdrawal of the outside third parties who have complicated the problem throughout its history because of their vested self-interests at the expense of Cypriots on both sides. This in turn requires that those at the *grassroots* level step up to the plate and seize control of their own destiny through an

---

[291] *See* Simon Bahceli, *Eroglu: "treated with contempt,"* CYPRUS MAIL, Sept. 19, 2010, http://www.cyprus-mail.com/cyprus/eroglu-treated-contempt/20100919 (last visited Oct. 9, 2010).

empowerment that will actively convert their historical culture of conflict to one of peace. This will permit the people on both sides to see each other through the mirror of *humanity*, enabling them to first mourn, followed by engagement in healing, then reconciling, and finally forging a new constructive story, abandoning any demonizing claims of who was wrong and who was harmed in historical recounts of what has gone before. In actuality, the *grassroots* element rather than the political elite holds the future in their hands because those on the ground are the ones who have the power to change the game through transformation of the conflict from the *bottom-up*. As was discussed earlier, the historical impasse has resulted from development of a Cypriot dual personality that must be faced.

The ineffective Cyprus "peace process" model must be replaced with an approach that actually has a chance of succeeding. Such a new approach needs to emanate from the grassroots level through education, training, and a commitment to seek a "just peace." Abandonment of the historical battle that sees the island's hotly contested factual history through the eyes of only one side, in favor of searching for *memories* that deal effectively with the past through present feelings in the everyday lives of ordinary Cypriots on both sides of the Green Line, must be the unified goal. Focus must shift to the sharing of such *memories* on both sides, so those psychological expressions will emanate from within members of each community themselves. This can be accomplished through an intense program establishing dialog groups island-wide empowering an honest exchange of *memories* from both sides of the Green Line that willingly admit the past transgressions of both communities, present the opportunity for apologies given and accepted, and grant forgiveness freely expressed so a true reconciliation can be achieved. The challenge presented is how to successfully disengage

177

from what the leadership on both sides has consistently advocated as separate positions that are incompatible. Is it realistic to expect that the current leaders (newly elected Greek Cypriot President Nicos Anastasiades and the beleaguered Turkish Cypriot Eroglu) can easily discard the historical baggage they and their respective predecessors have carried with such determination, to suddenly change course, asking their constituencies to cast off the effects of age-old propaganda in order to join together for peace? Will the ordinary people on both sides step up to take charge of their future during these extraordinary times before it is too late?

With the outbreak of citizen protest uprisings in Tunisia, Yemen, Egypt, Bahrain, Libya, Syria, and stirrings of discontent in Jordan, Saudi Arabia, Sudan and Zimbabwe, among a growing number of others, the world has changed drastically. Those in control can no longer rest easily continuing to employ their top-down elite political approach in governing citizens at the grassroots. While the Cyprus situation is not yet in the category of the protest uprisings in other parts of the world, the leaders of the two communities on the island would be prudent to look anew through fresh lenses at the problem that demands immediate solution. They must understand that they are answerable to the voices of the people on both sides of the Green Line who share courage and a belief that reunification is both possible and desirable.

Irrespective of the presence of the large number of Turkish troops in the northern part of the island, and assertions of the viability of the TRNC, the Republic of Cyprus, as originally formed in 1960 after gaining its independence from Great Britain, today legally encompasses the entire island. It was all too clear that if Christofias was not to be its "last President before partition,"[292] there had to be a dramatic change in the respective mindsets that were steeped in the blame constantly fanning the positional fires of contentious historical interpretation on both sides. This turned out not to be possible and, while UN-sponsored Cyprus reunification negotiations are technically continuing, the "stalemate" label looms overhead. To avoid this result, the parties must find a way to re-establish the necessary trust that has been lacking not only since the inception of the conflict but historically. A good starting point would be the inclusion of Track III representatives at the bargaining table to bring the force of reality to the likes of Anastasiades and Eroglu.

Although the interests of all concerned would be best realized by a negotiated complete settlement, current conditions do not bode well for such a successful outcome of the current negotiation process. Alternatively, it has been suggested that respective unilateral confidence-building steps should be taken by each side in areas such as the following, in order to create an environment that would encourage reaching a full final agreement at some point in the near future:[293]

- Turkey opening its ports and airports to Greek Cypriot sea and air traffic, along with permission to Greek Cypriot aircraft to transit Turkish airspace.

---

[292] *See* Nicos A. Rolandis, *I Look Out of the Window* (Sept. 15, 2010) (on file with author).

[293] *See* The International Crisis Group, *Cyprus: Six Steps toward a Settlement* (Feb, 22, 2011) (last visited July 9, 2011).

179

- Greek Cypriots allowing the port of Famagusta to handle all Cypriot (including Turkish Cypriot) trade with the EU, under Turkish Cypriot management and EU supervision; and permitting Green Line passage of Turkish goods so that Turkish Cypriots can also benefit.
- Returning the "ghost resort of Varosha" to its Greek Cypriot owners, subject to a UN interim regime that oversees reconstruction.
- Permitting charter flights to Turkish Cypriot Ercan Airport by Greek Cypriots and monitored by the EU.
- Devising a method to verify troop numbers on the island and organizing a census for the two communities to determine the exact population and their legal status.
- Cooperation between the administrative entities of both communities pending a political settlement.
- Steps taken by the European Commission to secure agreement on interim stages accompanied by avoidance of partisan statements during continuance of UN-sponsored talks, so that no one party is being clearly obstructive.

Muddying the waters is the fact that Turkey's accession to the EU appears to have lost its appeal to Turks both publically and politically, so that potential reunification of the island through Turkish efforts as the carrot-and-stick-approach no longer seems to be a key factor. Notwithstanding all this, and the opinion of at least one respected expert on the problem that while partition might be the "logical solution," reunification appears to be the foreseeable focus for negotiations,[294] the reality is that possible de jure partition of the island may provide the last wake-up call for the two sides to resolve their historical dispute. This was especially true at the time of the the then impending accession of the Greek Cypriot Republic of Cyprus to the EU presidency on July 1, 2012 for a term of six months.[295]

On the eve of what UN Secretary-General Ban Ki-Moon had indicated was a last attempt to reach a solution before a permanent partition of the island became a reality, there had been some discussion of the realistic view of the history of this conflict: A UN analysis for the period 1993-1998 showed a decrease in the number of Turkish Cypriots (dropping to 89,000 from 130,000) while at the same time the number of "settlers" from Turkey arriving on the island had reached 110,000 (up from 45,000), so that the native Turkish Cypriots were then "a minority within a minority," all to the end that Turkey through its settlers could make a legitimate case for its continued occupation of more than one-third (37%) of the island. This resulted in Turkish Cypriots being "outnumbered and out-voted" in their own part of the island. Reunification would bring with it hope to the Turkish Cypriots of achieving political equality at both the individual and community level with Greek Cypriots, so there would be no distinction concerning the

---

[294] Ker-Lindsay, James. *The Cyprus Problem: What Everyone Needs to Know.* New York: Oxford University Press, Inc., 2011.

[295] *See* Dorian Jones, *UN to Begin New Cyprus Unity Talks*, July 7, 2011, http://www.voanews.com/english/news/europe/ (last visited July 7, 2011).

rights enjoyed by members of each community. Included would be freedom of movement throughout the island.[296]

An argument has been made that as a member state of the EU, there is no longer any justification for Turkish troops to be present on the island that is internationally recognized as the Republic of Cyprus, especially since Turkey is an EU member "candidate country." On the other hand, it has been asserted that the de facto nature of the division of the island has resulted in a denial to Turkish Cypriots of the full benefit of EU membership already enjoyed by Greek Cypriots. Some fear that even if a bi-communal, bi-zonal federation is agreed to, the result will be a legitimization of "a separation obtained through the use of force" that will only serve the ego of Turkey. Notwithstanding the continual creation of bi-communal conferences and initiatives that could prove useful, it has been argued that Turkish Cypriots need to move their politicians away from the historical position that has left them "a minority within a community of Turkish settlers." In which case, from the bottom-up, they need to insist on "a European solution" through their right to participate "in a unified national Cypriot government" that will provide them with EU membership benefits and a "European solution as European citizens in partnership with the Greek Cypriots in a unified and civilized country." [297]

A key underlying topic that everyone involved with the Cyprus Problem is aware of, but which isn't discussed because it is considered to be uncomfortable, is that Greek Cypriots want a future that resembles a return to their past

---

[296] *See* Alfred A. Furrugia, *Comment: A federal constituent "state" is not in the interest of Turkish Cypriots*, FAMAGUSTA GAZETTE, July 6, 2011, http://famagusta-gazette.com/comment-a-federal-constituent-state-is-not-in-the-interest-of-turkish-cypriots (last visited July 7, 2011).

[297] *Ibid.*

control whereas Turkish Cypriots want one that mirrors the present "two-state" de facto partition. Each community leader and their policy makers feel the need to be tough in promoting the particular rights and interests of their respective communities while not giving in to the demands of the other. In the end, whatever the two leaders might be willing to agree to, they know that a prerequisite will be the holding of another referendum in each community approving a settlement on the basis that will be better for both sides than what they now have. Complicating this is the unanswered question of how much each community trusts the other to perform any agreement reached, in view of their respective "quasi-historical national narratives" and the uncertainty of how Turkey fits into the equation as it attempts to influence an ultimate settlement. Indicative of this was Turkey's pronouncements that (1) it would "freeze" its relations with the EU during the 2012 Greek Cypriot EU presidency unless the Cyprus conflict was resolved by that time;[298] and (2) if there were no solution by the end of 2011, there would be no further negotiations and the TRNC would continue to exist independently of the Greek Cypriots.[299] Added to this climate was the concern about possible Greek Cypriot "political and economic instability" resulting from the tragic accidental munitions blast in the south during July 2011 that destroyed the main

---

[298] *See* Semih Idiz, *Erdogan raises stakes on Cyprus, but will it work?* HURRIYET DAILY NEWS, July 24, 2011, http://www.hurriyetdailynews.com/n.php?n=erdogan-raises-stakes-on-cyprus-but-will-it-work-2011-07-21 (last visited July 23, 2011).

[299] *See* Mustafa Akyol, *Turkey on Cyprus: No More Mr. Nice Guy,* HURRIYET DAILY NEWS, July 24, 2011, http://rovere.ebay.com/rover/1/711-66992-24801-1/4 (last visited July 23, 2011).

power station on the island, requiring Greek Cypriots to obtain their electricity from Turkish Cypriots.[300]

What we ultimately have experienced is a situation where "deniers" in each community refuse to accept actual historical fact.[301] Successfully surmounting this obstacle will require thoughtful commitment on both sides by those in power and on the ground who, following years of uncertainty, must dare to dream and be willing to stand beside each other after remaining silent for so long, undertaking the burdensome task of working to effect the changes that will reunify the island before the stark reality of *de jure* partition sweeps across it.

In this respect, it may be the women on both sides who will ultimately make the difference. This is because my experience working with both communities demonstrated that, although there were key contributions by men, the women appeared to be the more dedicated in terms of making personal sacrifices while working for a solution and more willing than the men to assume and effectively perform leadership roles in bi-communal activities, even to the point of risking job security and placing their families second to such commitments. Perhaps this is indicative of the greater strength demonstrated by women in such circumstances.

The award of the 2011 Nobel Peace Prize to three women from Africa and the Middle East underscores these observations and provides a glimmer of hope for the eventual solution in Cyprus, if their Cypriot sisters can

---

[300] *See* Yonca Poyraz Dogan, *Analyst Hasguler: Greek Cyprus instability carries risks, opportunities for solving Cyprus conflict.* TODAY'S ZAMAN, August 8, 2011, http://www.todayszaman.com/news-252980-analyst-hasguler-greek-cyprus-instability-carries-risks-opportunities-for-solving-Cyprus-conflict-html.

[301] *See* Zenon Stavrinides, *Cyprus Negotiations: Searching for a Federal Settlement in a Divided Society* (on file with author).

follow these role models for others similarly struggling to improve their nations while advancing the importance of their gender rights. I have worked with such women in Cyprus on both sides of the Green Line who could turn the tide in favor of peaceful reunification of the island. Perhaps it is they who must step up to the plate, as uncharacteristic as this may seem for their culture.

Because of the desperate need for economic and social recovery on both sides of the Green Line, unprecedented bankruptcy facing the Republic of Cyprus exposing it to financial collapse as a result of its heavy exposure to the earlier Greek debt crisis through large holdings of Greek bonds,[302] and discovery of natural gas resources in the eastern Mediterranean very backyard of Cypriots, this may well be the last remaining opportunity for the reunification solution that has eluded both sides from inception of the current division.[303] Restricted access to bank accounts and imposition of capital controls, drying up of trade credit, plunging automobile sales, and a drop in tourism that is the island's number one industry, all seem to be making the 2013 EU financial bailout a bad deal for Greek Cypriots.[304]

There appears to be sentiment for taking a second look at reunification in terms of the potential source of growth available in the context of the eastern

---

[302] *See* Dylan Matthews, *Everything you need to know about the Cyprus bailout, in one FAQ*, WONKBLOG, Mar. 18, 2013, available at http://www.washingtonpost.com/blogs/wonkblog/wp/2013/03/18/every hting-you-need-to-know-about-the-Cyprus-bailout-in-one-FAQ (last visited May 31, 2013).

[303] *See* Loucas Charalambous, *Games of history: A solution would suit us now,* CYPRUS MAIL, May 12, 2013.

[304] *See The Cypriot economy: Through a glass, darkly.* THE ECONOMIST, Apr. 27, 2013, available at http://www.economist.com/news/finance-and-economics/21576666 (last visited Apr. 28, 2013).

Mediterranean Aphrodite gas field and the revenue potential presented by the tourism industry. Both of these require a reunified island.[305] The gas field deposits involving Turkey, Cyprus, Israel, Lebanon, and possibly Syria, have been estimated to be equal to the annual total consumption of the world's natural gas. This presents an additional wild card that must be considered.[306]

While there has been speculation that Turkey would weigh in to assist in solving the problem by using its influence with Turkish Cypriots, this has become questionable as a result of the thousands of Turkish protestors demonstrating in their country against what they see as the authoritarian government of Prime Minister Recep Tayyip Erdogan. A simple announcement by Erdogan's government concerning plans to demolish a public park in Istanbul to make way for new construction ignited the protests that spread to Turkey's capital of Ankara and other major Turkish cities, bringing to the fore what has been seen as the conflict between his conservative religious mores and a country governed by secular laws. In addition to opposing the loss of the park, demonstrators have demanded early elections and Erdogan's resignation. Although he has changed the demolition plans, his governing AK party has rejected the call for early elections.[307]

---

[305] See *Cyprus: Divided they fall*. THE ECONOMIST, Apr. 27, 2013, available at http://www.economist.com/news/leaders/21576676-outlook-cyprus-dire-time-think-again (last visited Apr. 28, 2013).

[306] See *Cyprus celebrates independence with no solution in sight*. SOUTHERN DAILY PRESS, June 16, 2013, available at http://southerndailypress.com/cyprus-celebrates-independence-with-no-solution-in-sight (last visited June 15, 2013).

[307] See *Turkey protestors clash with police as demonstrations enter 10th day*. Voice of America, June 08, 2013, available at http://www.voanews.com/articleprintview/1678101.html (last visited June 8, 2013).

Meanwhile, because of a successful no-confidence censure motion against Turkish Cypriot Prime Minister Irsen Kucuk, engineered by the three main opposition parties, Eroglu was forced to appoint Sibel Siber (the first female Turkish Cypriot political leader) to head a caretaker government until the next scheduled election that is anticipated to be held as early as 2014. Kucuk had been backed by Erdogan, who was believed to be planning to weaken or replace Eroglu, who is not up for re-election until 2015. The disaffection between Erdogan and Eroglu apparently resulted from their 2004 split concerning the reunification referendum and the Annan Plan. It seems that Erdogan was in favor of the referendum but Eroglu lobbied against it. In the 2010 presidential contest between Eroglu and former Turkish Cypriot leader Mehmet Ali Talat, Erdogan backed Talat.[308]

Rolandis, the former Greek Cypriot government minister, has urged consideration of the probability that the natural gas could be the island's "strong, very last hope" for the economy as well as solution of the Cyprus Problem.[309] One important Turkish Cypriot academic viewpoint is that a bi-zonal, bi-communal federation is the only possible way out of this morass because it will resolve the property issue, the hydrocarbons will be controlled and jointly run by Turkish and Greek Cypriots, and provide the basis for an "amicable divorce" in the event reunification subsequently fails.[310]

---

[308] See Editors, *Global Insider: Turkey's hand seen in collapse of northern Cyprus government.* WORLD POLITICS REVIEW, June 19, 2013, available at http://www.worldpoliticsreview.com/articles/print/13032 (last visited June 19, 2013).

[309] See Nicos A. Rolandis, *Following the Legacies of Plato and Karamanlis* (Mar. 13, 2013) (on file with the author).

[310] See Ahmet Sozen, *Solving Cyprus by blending Idealism with Pragmatism,* in RESOLVING CYPRUS: NEW APPROACHES TO

But again the forces of a divisive island prevail with only the playing field having been changed from the historical logjam to the natural gas deposits and present financial crisis that begs for a solution through reunification. Characteristically, Turkish Cypriots seem anxious to reach an accommodation while Greek Cypriots insist on dealing with their failing economy before they return to the underlying issue of reunification, declaring firmly that the financial crisis will not cause them to capitulate in connection with what they have required for reunification.[311] On the other hand, the resolve of Turkish Cypriots to achieve a solution has been clouded by the growing public discontent with the administration of Eroglu, resulting in a political deadlock that Turkey has declared must be solved.[312] It is a historical repeat with only the clothing having been changed; leaving one to wonder whether there will ever be a resolution.

CONFLICT RESOLUTION (James Ker-Lindsay, ed., forthcoming 2014, I.B. Tauris).

[311] *See* Nicos Bellos, *Cyprus will not cave in on Cyprus issue because of crisis, says Mavroyiannis,* FAMAGUSTA GAZETTE, May 16, 2013, available at http://famagusta-gazette.com/cyprus-will-not-cave-in-on-cyprus-issue-because-of-crisis (last visited May 17, 2013).

[312] *See* Selim Akan, *Solve political deadlock: Ankara to Turkish Cypriots,* HURRIYET DAILY NEWS, May 30, 2013, available at http://www.hurriyetdailynews.com/solve-political-deadlock-ankara-to-turkish-cyprus.aspx (last visited May 30, 2013).

Appendix A[313]

The Oslo I Declaration

OSLO GROUP DECLARATION ON CYPRUS "A five-day workshop took place in Oslo, Norway, between twenty-five Greek-Cypriots and twenty-five Turkish-Cypriots in their individual capacities. They came together at the invitation of the Cyprus Fulbright Commission and were hosted by that organization and the PRIO International Peace Research Institute.

"The need for this meeting in Oslo resulted from the difficulties currently faced by people not being able to meet on the island. The aim was to promote better understanding, increased contacts, resumption of bicommunal [sic] activities, and to provide ideas for more community involvement in relation to the Cyprus problem.

"During the meetings, communication skills were acquired and practiced setting the stage for an exchange of views on the solution to the Cyprus problem and the future of the bicommunal [sic] movement.

"In relation to the Cyprus problem the group emphasized the importance of working towards the establishment of a democratic, bizonal [sic] bicommunal [sic] Federal Republic in which human rights will be recognized and implemented, the security needs of both communities will be safeguarded, and which will achieve membership in the European Union as the Federal Republic of Cyprus at the earliest possible time.

---

[313] *See* TURK, *supra* note 36, at 225.

189

"The group expressed anxiety over the current deterioration of the peace efforts and escalation of tension on the island. It is believed that the resumption and support by every body of bicommunal [sic] contacts would play an important role in creating a conducive climate for cooperation and understanding, which will form the basis for a fair, just, and lasting peace in Cyprus.

"The necessity of reconvening the Oslo group was recognized by the participants for further discussion of the issues relating to coexistence development activities. It is hoped that these [discussions] will promote better understanding in Cyprus and facilitate a speedy solution to the Cyprus problem.

"The group would like to express their appreciation to the Cyprus Fulbright Commission, the PRIO International Peace Research Institute, and the Norwegian Foreign Ministry for making this event possible. - Oslo, Norway July 4, 1998."

Appendix B[314]

Annan Plan for Cyprus

Annan Plan for Cyprus Settlement,
http://www.tcea.org.uk/Annan-Plan-ForCyprus-Settlement.htm.

Main points of the Annan Plan:
1. A single state comprised of two equal components in a dissoluble union
2. A single international entity offering a single Cypriot citizenship
3. Territorial adjustments reducing Turkish Cypriot component of the island to 28.5% from 36%
4. Return of 85,000 Greek Cypriot refugees to their homes in the island's Turkish Cypriot north
5. Cyprus to join the European Union and maintain special links to Greece and Turkey
6. A two-chamber parliament, each containing 48 members
7. A six-member presidential council proportional to the population of the two states, with a 10-month rotating presidency
8. Demilitarization of the island, reinforced by an embargo on arms imports
9. Constitutional safeguards for civil and minority rights

---

[314] *Ibid.* at 247.

Appendix C[315]

Workshop Ground Rules

"JUNE PEACEBUILDING WORKSHOP NUMBER TWO RULES GOVERNING DISCUSSION OF THE ANNAN PLAN"

— Please practice empowerment and recognition
— Please be courteous, wait for the prior speaker to fully conclude, do not interrupt
— Please speak only when you have something NEW to add...DO NOT REPEAT what others have said. before you...AND REMEMBER: 'I' STATEMENTS
— Please be patient and wait for your turn to speak. You will be recognized eventually for that purpose, and you will have the opportunity to express yourself
— Please express YOUR PERSONAL VISION regarding the possible content of the Plan
— Please consider the respective interests and underlying needs involved rather than positions...AND REMEMBER: ALL THE PRINCIPLES OF HUMANISTIC CONFLICT MANAGEMENT
— Please be persuasive and not coercive
— Please be collaborative rather than confrontational
— Please make it all work
— Please keep in mind that each of you CAN make a difference. "GOAL: To create a possible grassroots alternate plan by consensus that you feel could work to solve the Cyprus problem."

---

[315] *Ibid.*

192

Appendix D[316]

Workshop Possible Peace Issues

JUNE 2003 PEACEBUILDING WORKSHOP NUMBER
TWO***
*LIST OF POSSIBLE PEACE PLAN ISSUES FOR
AGENDA"*

1 All people on Cyprus living together in peace
2 Long-term vision of future for Cyprus
3 Provision for periodic revisions of plan
4 Return of displaced persons from each community
5 Immediate removal of all barriers, embargoes, and complete freedom of movement for all people on Cyprus without showing passports
6 Equal rights (human and otherwise) and opportunities for all people on Cyprus
7 Balancing property rights with the right of shelter
8 Demilitarization
9 Definition of 'just and lasting solution to Cyprus problem'
10 Procedure to guarantee endurance of a dissoluble union
11 Exercise of political rights for citizens at both state and federal levels
12 A single state comprised of two equal units
13 Freedom of settlement without limitation
14 Proportionate representation should reflect the population of the two communities
15 Structure and term of presidency
16 Turkish Cypriot state to continue with current name with current geographical boundaries
17 Respect for international agreements

---

[316] *Ibid.* at 247-248.

18 Territorial adjustments
19 European Union membership and special links to Greece and Turkey
20 Definition of terms to be used
21 Adoption of law of the European Union as the basis for the laws of Cyprus
22 Common education facilities [modified during discussion to include 'one version of revised history; bi-communal respect for tolerance, diversity, and ethnicity']
23 Common health facilities
24 Control of airspace
25 Ways of removing [modified during discussion to include 'animosity, hostility, and'] ill feelings between the two communities
26 Unified state without discrimination
27 Elections and voting structure
28 Trade rights and agreements
29 Legitimacy of European Union accession
30 How to learn not to 'bury future in the past'
31 Eurovision selection process for Cyprus
32 Mainland Turks
33 Civil and criminal court structure with two-state jurisdiction
34 Effect of no solution to Cyprus problem by May 2004
35 No links to Turkey or Greece and no guarantors or British Bases
36 Establishment of an Office for Mediation
37 Cyprus and Turkey to become European Union members at the same time
38 Bicommunality [sic] and bizonality [sic]
39 Citizenship and identity
40 Rights of other minorities on Cyprus
41 Areas of responsibility between federal and state entities and their functionality

42 Two separate states
43 Rights of subsequent purchasers
44 Global exchange and compensation
45 Revisiting 1960 Zurich Agreement
46 Interdependent economic system
47 Free labor movement and freedom to choose employment
48 Bicommunal [sic] youth centers

In the order to be discussed, the following numbered issues from the list of 48 were selected: 6, 8, 25, 5, 22, 13, 32, 34, 1, and 21. The five of the ten issues discussed and voted on were numbers 6, 8, 25, 5, 22. While the purpose of this discussion does not extend to an analysis of the results of the voting, it should be noted that the overwhelming majority of votes supported positive solutions.

Appendix E[317]

RockRose Institute

This information was provided by Dr. Dilek Latif who was an instructor in the International Relations Department at Near East University in North Nicosia (Turkish Cypriot), Cyprus, and was a visiting Fulbright Scholar in the Negotiation, Conflict Resolution and Peacebuilding Program at California State University, Dominguez Hills, for the spring 2007 semester. In an e-mail to the author, dated March 19, 2007, Dr. Latif noted:

"The RockRose Institute Youth Dialogue Project (YDP) is engaged youth (ages 18-24) from five countries Cyprus, New Zealand, South Africa, Denmark and United States. Six youth were selected to represent each of these countries (in case of Cyprus 3 Turkish Cypriots and 3 Greek Cypriots), based on their role as change-makers in their communities and their on-going commitment to non-violence. The students have been learning and practicing skills of inquiry, dialogue and conflict resolution. Since November 2006, participants attended in a series of four in-country meetings to learn and practice dialogue using the different methodologies: The World Café, Public Conversations Project, Search for Common Ground, and Facing History and Ourselves. The Project will end in May 2007.

"During the Search for Common Ground meeting that took place on 5th of January 2007 at the Near East University Library in north Nicosia the Cypriot youth focused on finding a common ground for Cyprus. The team

---

[317] *See* TURK, *supra* note 94, at 500-501.

196

discussed: 'What can be our common ground? Can Cypriotness be our common ground? Are we Turks, Greeks, Cypriots, Turkish Cypriots or Greek Cypriots? It is very complicated to identify ourselves. We know that we are different than the mainland Turks and mainland Greeks. How do we define ourselves: Turkish Speaking or Greek Speaking Cypriots?' At the end, the session ended with the outcome that Cypriotness is our common ground and we can use this to re-unite our island and identify ourselves as Turkish Speaking and Greek Speaking Cypriots in Cyprus.

"Dr. Dilek Latif is one of the Turkish Cypriots [sic] facilitators of the Cyprus team alongside [sic] Mehves Beyidoglu Onen, [and] Dr. Stavroula Philippou and Dr. Miranda Christou [are the Greek Cypriot facilitators].

"For more information about the project please visit http://www.rockroseinstitute.org."

Email from Dr. Dilek Latif, Instructor, Near East U., N. Nicosia (Turkish Cypriot), to author (Mar. 19, 2007, 00:00:00 PST) (on file with author).

197

BIBLIOGRAPHY

Akan, Selim. 2013. "Solve political deadlock: Ankara to Turkish Cypriots," *HURRIYET DAILY NEWS*, May 30. http://www.hurriyetdailynews.com/solve-political-deadlock-ankara-to-turkish-cyprus.aspx (last visited May 30, 2013).

Akyol, Mustafa. 2011. "Turkey on Cyprus: No More Mr. Nice Guy," *HURRIYET DAILY NEWS*, July 24. http://rovere.ebay.com/rover/1/711-66992-24801-1/4 (last visited July 23, 2011).

Allan, Pierre, and Alexis Keller. 2006. "The Concept of a Just Peace, or Achieving Peace through Recognition, Renouncement, and Rule." In *What Is a Just Peace?* eds. Pierre Allan and Alexis Keller. New York: Oxford University Press.

Anastasakis, Othon, et al. 2004. "Getting to Yes: Suggestions for Embellishment of the Annan Plan for Cyprus." http://www.sant.ox.ac.uk/esc/esc-lectures/Oxford_Cyprus.pdf.

Anastasiou, Harry. 2008. *The Broken Olive Branch: Nationalism, Ethnic Conflict, and the Quest for Peace in Cyprus. Vol. 2 Nationalism versus Europeanization. Syracuse: Syracuse Uni*versity Press.

Annan Plan. 2004. "Report of the Secretary General on his Mission of Good Offices in Cyprus," UN doc. S/2004/437 of 28 May 2004.

Anonymous. 2004. "Secretary-General's Visit to Burgenstock, Switzerland," March 28-31. http://www.un.org/av/ photo/sgtrips/sgswitz032804.htm (last visited Apr. 28, 2007).

Anonymous. "EU Pledges AID for Turkish Cyprus." *BBC News*.http://newsnote.bbc.co.wk/mpapps/pagetools/print/ne ws.bbc.co.uk/1/hi/world/europe/3660 (last visited Oct. 9, 2005).

Anonymous. 2005. "Turkish Cypriots Elect New President," *The Los Angeles Times*, April 18:A6.

Anonymous. "UN to Revive Cyprus Talks in May."*EU News, Policy Positions & EU Actors online. EurActiv.com* –http://www.euractiv.com/ Article?tcmuri=tcm:29-152089-16&type=News (last visited Feb. 8, 2006).

Anonymous. 2006. "The Cyprus Stalemate: What Next?" *The International Crisis Group.* March 8, http://www.crisisgroup.org/home/index.cfm?id=4003&l=1.

Anonymous. 2006. "E.U. Wrangles over Turkish Initiative." *FRANCE 24*.December 8. http://www.france24.com/france24Public/en/news/Eur ope/20061206-Cyprus-Reax.html.

Anonymous. 2007. "Cyprus President Against Casino." *FIN. MIRROR*, January 18. http://www.financialmirror.com/more_news.php?id=5854 &type=news.

Anonymous. 2007. "Talat: We Want the World to Take Notice of Turkish Cypriots More and Lift the Unfair Isolations." *ANATOLIAN TIMES* (Turk.). January 23. http://www.anatoliantimes.com/hbr2.asp?id=160277.

Anonymous. 2007. "Talat Letter to Ban Ki-Moon: Turkish Cypriots Have Equal Right on Natural Resources."*CYPRUS OBSERVER*, February 9. http://www.observercyprus.com/ observer/NewsDetails.aspx?id=1154.

Anonymous. "Tragic Common Ground Between North and South."*CYPRUS MAIL.* http://www.cyprus-mail.com/news/main.php?id=30470&cat_id=1 (last visited Feb. 23, 2007).

Anonymous. 2007. "A Timeline of Key Events in Cyprus' History." INTERNATIONAL HERALD TRIBUNE, March 9. http://www.iht.com/articles/ap/2007/03/09/europe/EU-GEN-Cyprus-Timeline.php.

Anonymous. 2007. "Cyprus' Greek Side Razes Part of Barrier." *The Los Angeles Times*, March 9: A9.

Anonymous. 2008. "Cyprus: Reversing the Drift to Partition." EUROPE REPORT NO. 190, *International Crisis Group,* January 10. http://www.crisisgroup.org/home/index.cfm?id=5945&1=1 (last visited June 9, 2009).

Anonymous. *Will the Governing Coalition in Cyprus Collapse? GR REPORTER*, April 13. http://www.grreporter.info/en/node/645.

Anonymous. 2009. "UK Court Says No to Direct Flights to the North,"*CYPRUS MAIL*, July 29. http://www.cyprus-mail.com/news/main.php?id=47057&cat_id=1.

Anonymous. 2011."Cyprus: Six Steps toward a Settlement," *The International Crisis Group*, February 22. (last visited July 9, 2011).

Anonymous. 2013. "Cyprus: Divided they fall." THE ECONOMIST, Apr. 27. http://www.economist.com/news/leaders/21576676-outlook-cyprus-dire-time-think-again (last visited Apr. 28, 2013).

Anonymous. 2013. "The Cypriot economy: Through a glass, darkly." THE ECONOMIST, Apr. 27. http://www.economist.com/news/finance-and-economics/21576666 (last visited Apr. 28, 2013).

Anonymous. 2013. *"Turkey protestors clash with police as demonstrations enter 10th day,"* Voice of America, June 08. http://www.voanews.com/articleprintview/1678101.html (last visited June 8, 2013).

Anonymous. 2013. *"Cyprus celebrates independence with no solution in sight,"* SOUTHERN DAILY PRESS, June 16. http://southerndailypress.com/cyprus-celebrates-independence-with-no-solution-in-sight (last visited June 15, 2013).

Attalides, Michael. 1979. *Cyprus: Nationalism and International Politics.* New York: St. Martin's Press.

Bahceli, Simon. 2009. "Peace is Too Important to be Left to Politicians,"*CYPRUS MAIL*, April 2009. http://www.cyprus-mail.com/news/main.php?id=46669&_id=1 (last visited July 7, 2009).

Bahceli, Simon. 2010. "Eroglu: 'treated with contempt,'"*CYPRUS MAIL*, September. 19. http://www.cyprus-mail.com/cyprus/eroglu-treated-contempt/20100919 (last visited Oct. 9, 2010).

Baier-Allen, Susanne. 2004. "The Failure of Power-Sharing in Cyprus: Causes and Consequences." In *Managing and Settling Ethnic Conflicts,* eds. Ulrich Schneckener and Stefan Wolff, 77-91, 262-280.

Bellos, Nicos. 2013. *"Cyprus will not cave in on Cyprus issue because of crisis, says Mavroyiannis,"* FAMAGUSTA GAZETTE, May 16. http://famagusta-gazette.com/cyprus-will-not-cave-in-on-cyprus-issue-because-of-crisis (last visited May 17, 2013).

Biggar, Nigel. 2003. "Conclusion." In *Burying the Past: Making Peace and Doing Justice after Civil Conflict,* (ed.) Nigel Biggar, 309-313. Washington, D.C.: Georgetown University Press.

Braithwaite, John. 2002. *Restorative Justice and Responsive Regulation.* New York: Oxford University Press.

Brey, Hansjoreg, and Claudia Muller, eds. 1993. *Insight Guides: Cyprus.* Auckland: APA Publications Pte Ltd.

Buckley, Richard, ed. 1998. *Greece, Turkey, Cyprus: Triangle of Conflict – and Opportunity.* London: European Schoolbooks Limited.

Burgess, Heidi, Guy Burgess, and Sandra Kaufman. 2006. "The Challenge of Intractable Conflicts: Introduction to the Colloquium," *Conflict Resolution Quarterly* 24:174.

Bush, Robert A. Baruch, and Joseph P. Folger. 1994. *The Promise of Mediation: Responding to Conflict through Empowerment and Recognition.* San Francisco: Jossey-Bass.

Byrne, Sean J. 2006. "The Roles of External Ethnoguarantors and Primary Mediators in Cyprus and Northern Ireland," *Conflict Resolution Quarterly* 24: 149, 165.

Calotychos, Vangelis, ed. 1998. *Cyprus and Its People: Nation, and Experience in an Unimaginable Community, 1955-1997.* Boulder: Westview Press.

Camp, Glenn D. 1980. "Greek-Turkish Conflict over Cyprus," *Political Science Quarterly,* 95, 3:49.

Charalambous, Loucas. "Return to Point Zero," *CYPRUS MAIL.* http://www.cyprus-mail.com/news/main.php?id=31087&cat_id=1 (last visited Mar. 6, 2007).

Charalambous, Loucas. 2009. *"President's Handling of Talks Hardly Inspires Confidence,"* CYPRUS MAIL, January 18. http://www.cyprus-mail.com/news/main.php?id=43585&cat_id=1.

Charalambous, Loucas. 2013. *"Games of history: A solution would suit us now,* CYPRUS MAIL, May 12.

Christou, Jean. 2002. "Oslo Group Slams its Critics," *Cyprus Mail: News Articles in English,* February 15. http://www.hri.org/news/cyprus/cmnews/2002/0202-15.cmnews.html.

Cloke, Kenneth. 2008. *Conflict Revolution: Mediating Evil, War, Injustice and Terrorism.* Santa Ana: Janis Publications.

Coleman, Peter T. 2006. "Intractable Conflict." In *The Handbook of Conflict Resolution Theory and Practice,* (Ed) Morton Deutsch, 533-555. San Francisco: Jossey-Bass.

Coughlan, Reed. 2000. "Cyprus: From Corporate Autonomy to the Search for Territorial Federalism. In *Autonomy and Ethnicity: Negotiating Competing Claims in Multi-Ethnic States,* ed. Yash Ghai, 219-239. Cambridge: Cambridge University Press.

Crawshaw, Nancy. 1978. *The Cyprus Revolt: An Account of the Struggle for Union with Greece.* London: Allen and Unwin.

Cyprus Press and Information Office: Turkish Cypriot Press Review Directory. 2002. "Threatening E-mails to the Turkish Cypriot Members of the Oslo Group."

http://www.hri.org/news/cyprus/tcpr/2002/02-02-11.tcpr.html.

De Cuellar, Javier. 1997. *Pilgrimage for Peace: A Secretary-General's Memoir.* London: Palgrave Macmillan.

Demir Gul, and Niki Gamm. 2007. "Rauf Denktas: 'Politics Was Not My Choice'."*TURKISH DAILY TIMES,* February 3, http://www.turkishdailynews.com.tr/article.php?enewsid=65303.

De Trense, Max. 2009. "Challenge to Ban on Direct Flights to Northern Cyprus Will Be Heard in High Court,"*SYSCON Media, Inc.*, April 17. 2009, http://www.syscon.com/node/924037

Deutsch, Morton. 2006. "Justice and Conflict." In *The Handbook of Conflict Resolution Theory and Practice,* ed. Morton Deutsch, 62-64. San Francisco: Jossey-Bass.

Diamond, Louise, and John W. McDonald. 1996. *Multi-Track Diplomacy: A Systems Approach to Peace.* 3rd ed. West Hartford: Kumarian Press.

Dogan, Yonca Poyraz. 2011. "Analyst Hasguler: Greek Cyprus instability carries risks, opportunities for solving Cyprus conflict."*TODAY'S ZAMAN*, August 8. http://www.todayszaman.com/news-252980-analyst-hasguler-greek-cyprus-instability-carries-risks-opportunities-for-solving-Cyprus-conflict-html.

Editors. 2013. Global Insider: "Turkey's hand seen in collapse of northern Cyprus government." WORLD POLITICS REVIEW, June 19. http://www.worldpoliticsreview.com/articles/print/13032 (last visited June 19, 2013).

Ehrlich, Thomas. 1974. *Cyprus, 1958-1967: International Crises and the Role of Law.* New York: Oxford University Press.

Evripidou, Stefanos. 2009. "Christofias More Optimistic After Talks than Before," *CYPRUS MAIL*, February 13. http://www.cyprus-mail.com/news/main.php?id=44010&cat_id=1.

Evripidou, Stefanos . 2009. *"The Talks: One Year On,"* CYPRUS MAIL, Aug. 30. http://www.cyprus-mail.com/news/main.php?id=47548&_id=1 (last visited Sept. 20, 2009).

Fisher, Roger et al. *Beyond Machiavelli.* New York: Penguin.

Focus Information Agency. 2009. "Today Most of Turkish Cypriots Would Reject Annan Plan: Poll," March 5. http://www.focus-fen.net (last visited March 5, 2009) (on file with author).

Focus Information Agency. 2009. "U.S. Does Not Plan to Impose Solution to Cyprus Issue. " April 23. http://www.focus-fen.net (last visited May 5, 2009) (on file with author).

Foundation for Co-Existence (FCE): "Promoting Coexistence through Human Security," http://www.fcoex.com/pages/glossary.htm (last visited Sept. 1, 2005).

Furrugia, Alfred A. 2011. "Comment: A federal constituent 'state' is not in the interest of Turkish Cypriots,"*FAMAGUSTA GAZETTE*, July 7. http://famagusta-gazette.com/comment-a-federal-constituent-state-is-not-in-the-interest-of-turkish-cypriots (last visited July 7, 2011).

Gültali, Selcuk. 2007. "Greek Cypriots Fear Kosovo May Set Precedent for Northern Cyprus," *TODAY'S ZAMAN*, March 20. http://www.todayszaman.com/tz-web/detaylar.do?load=detay&link=105722.

Hannay, David. 2005. *Cyprus: The Search for a Solution*. London: I.B. Tauris & Co. Ltd.

Holland, Robert. 1998. *Britain and the Revolt in Cyprus*. Oxford: Clarendon Press.

Idiz, Semih. 2011. "Erdogan raises stakes on Cyprus, but will it work?" *HURRIYET DAILY NEWS*, July 24. http://www.hurriyetdailynews.com/n.php?n=erdogan-raises-stakes-on-cyprus-but-will-it-work-2011-07-21 (last visited July 23, 2011).

Int'l Crisis Group, The Cyprus Stalemate: What Next?, Mar. 8, 2006, http://www.crisisgroup.org/home/index.cfm?id=4003&l=1.

International Crisis Group, *Cyprus: Reversing the Drift to Partition* 1, EUROPE REPORT NO. 190, Jan. 10, 2008, http://www.crisisgroup.org/home/index.cfm?id=5945&1=1 (last visited June 9, 2009).

James, Alan. 2002. *Keeping the Peace in the Cyprus Crisis of 1963-64*. London: Palgrave.

Jarstad, Anna. 2001. "Changing the Game: Consociational Theory and Ethnic Quotas in Cyprus and New Zealand." *Uppsala University, Department of Peace and Conflict Research, Report* 58:165.

Jones, Dorian.2011. "UN to Begin New Cyprus Unity Talks, "July 7, http://www.voanews.com/english/news/europe/ (last visited July 7, 2011).

Jones, L.W. St. John. 1983. *The Population of Cyprus.* London: Maurice Temple Smith.

Joseph, Joseph S. 1997. *Cyprus: Ethnic Conflict and International Politics (from Independence to the Threshold of the European Union.* 2nd ed. London: Palgrave Macmillan.

Ker-Lindsay, James. 2005. *EU Accession and UN Peacemaking in Cyprus.* New York: Palgrave Macmillan.

Ker-Lindsay, James. 2011. *The Cyprus Problem: What Everyone Needs to Know.* New York: Oxford University Press.

Kilic, Ali Aslan. 2007. "Experts Suggest Removal of UN Peacekeeping Force in Cyprus," *TODAY'S ZAMAN,* March. 10. http://www.todayszaman.com/tz-web/detaylar.do?load=detay&=105048.

Kizilyurek, Niyazi. 2009. "Cyprus Silently Begins Year 2009." *CYPRUS OBSERVER*, January 9. http://www.observercyprus.com/observer/NewsDetails.aspx?id=3382#.

Lederach, John Paul. 2003. *The Little Book of Conflict Transformation.* Intercourse: Good Books.

Macdonald, R. St.J. 1981. "International Law and the Conflict on Cyprus," *Canadian Yearbook of International Law* 29:3-49.

MacNair, Rachel M. 2003. *The Psychology of Peace: An Introduction.* Westport: Praeger.

Markides, Diana Weston. 2001. "Cyprus 1957-1963, From Colonial Conflict to Constitutional Crisis: The Key Role of the Municipal Issue."*University of Minnesota, Minnesota Mediterranean and East European Monograph*, 8:187-188.

Matthew, Jennie. 2002. "Conflict Resolution Critics 'Playing a Political Game,'" *Cyprus Mail: News Articles in English,* January 29. http://www.hri.org/news/cyprus/cmnews/2002/02-01-29.cmnews.html.

Matthews, Dylan. 2013. " *Everything you need to know about the Cyprus bailout, in one FAQ,"* WONKBLOG, Mar. 18. http://www.washingtonpost.com/blogs/wonkblog/wp/2013/03/18/everyhting-you-need-to-know-about-the-Cyprus-bailout-in-one-FAQ (last visited May 31, 2013).

McCormack, Sean. 2007. Spokesman, U.S. Dep't of State, *Daily Press Briefing,* January 10. (transcript available at http://www.state.gov/r/pa/prs/dpb/2007/78512.htm).

Mehmet, Ozay. 2009. "Guest Comment: The End of the Cyprus Problem," FinancialMirror.com, February 19. http://www.financialmirror.com/Columnist/COMMENT/262

Miall, Hugh et al. (1999). Contemporary *Conflict Resolution.*

Misra, S.S. 1997. "Ethnic Conflict in Cyprus: A Socio-Political Study." *In Cyprus: In Search of Peace and Justice,* (ed.) R.C. Sharma & Stavros A. Epaminond, 198-205. Canberra: Somali Publications.

Moore, Christopher. 2003. *The Mediation Process: Practical Strategies for Resolving Conflict.* San Francisco: Jossey-Bass.

Morgan, Tabitha. "Cyprus Keeps its Hidden Barrier." *BBC News (United Kingdom).* http://news.bbc.co.uk/1/hi/world/europe/4313016.stm (last visited Oct. 7, 2005).

Nye, Joseph. S. Jr. 2007. *Understanding International Conflicts: An Introduction to Theory and History.* White Plains: Pearson/Longman.

Ozgur, Ozdemir A. "Comment - The Cyprus Problem: Ideas, Realities and Might 2." http://www.cyprus-mail.com/news/main.php?id=18989&cat_id=1 (last visited Sep. 1, 2005).

Palley, Claire. 2005. *An International Relations Debacle: The UN Secretary-General's Mission of Good Offices in Cyprus 1999-2004.* Oxford: Hart Publishing.

Papadakis, Yiannis. 2005. *Echoes From The Dead Zone: Across The Cyprus Divide.* London: I.B. Tauris & Co. Ltd.

Pickering, Paula M. 2007. *Peacebuilding in the Balkans: The View from the Ground Floor.* New York: Cornell University Press.

Pope, Hugh. 2008. "Cyprus: Things are Looking Up," *INTERNATIONAL CRISIS GROUP*, September 17. http://www.crisisgroup.org/home/index.cfm?id=5731&1=1 (last visited June 9, 2009).

Pope, Hugh, 2010. "Waiting for Miracles on Cyprus," *CURRENT HISTORY (International Crisis Group)*, March 15. http://www.crisisgroup.org/home/index.cfm?id=6582&1=1 (last visited March 19, 2010)

Purcell, H. D. 1968. *Cyprus.* New York: Praeger.

Rehn, Ollie. 1995. Member, European Commission, Responsible for Enlargement. Speech at the Cyprus International Conference Center. In *Cyprus: One Year After Accession.*

http://europa.eu.int/comm/commission_barroso/rehn/speec
hes/pdf/050513_nicosia.pdf.

Rolandis, Nicos A. "King Jigme and Floundering Cyprus." http://www.cyprus-mail.com/news/main.php?id=24591&cat_id=1 (last visited Feb. 26, 2006).

Rolandis, Nicos A. 2006. "Cyprus: Political Due Diligence 2004-2006; The Gods and Friedrich Schiller," December 28. (on file with author).

Rolandis, Nicos A. 2007. "Greek Hero Kolokotronis, The Gunshot and the New President," January 18. (on file with author).

Rolandis, Nicos A. 2009. "After So Many 'No's,' Shall We Whisper 'Yes, We Can'?" *CYPRUS MAIL,* January 11. http://www.cyprus-mail.com/news/main.php?id=43451&archive=1. .

Rolandis, Nicos A. 2009. "The Beautiful People, Enosis, Partition . . . and Our Bloody Mess." *CYPRUS MAIL,* February 15. http://www.cyprus-mail.com/news/main.php?id=44065&archive=1

Rolandis, Nicos A. 2010. "I Look Out of the Window," September 15. (on file with author).

Rolandis, Nicos A. 2013. "Following the Legacies of Plato and Karamanlis," Mar. 13. (on file with author).

Rothman, Jay. 1997. *Resolving Identity-Based Conflict in Nations, Organizations, and Communities.* San Francisco: Jossey-Bass.

Ryan, Stephen. 2007. *The Transformation of Violent Intercommunal Conflict.* Burlington: Ashgate Publishing Company.

Sariibrahimoglu, Lale. 2007. "Two-State Solution for Cyprus?"*TODAY'S ZAMAN*, February 1. http://www.todayszaman.com/tz-web/yazarDetay.do?haberno=101616.

Sariibrahimoglu, Lale. 2007. "Negotiated Partition: An Ideal Solution for Cyprus."*TODAY'S ZAMAN*, March 6. http://www.todayszaman.com/tz-web/yazarDetay.do? haberno=104603.

Saunders, Harold H. 1999. *A Public Peace Process: Sustained Dialogue to Transform Racial and Ethnic Conflicts*. New York: Palgrave Macmillan.

Savvides, Philippos. 2004. "Written Evidence Submitted by Dr. Philippos Savvides, Research Fellow,"*Hellenic Foundation for European and Foreign Policy (ELIAMEP)*, October 17. http://www.publications.parliament.uk/pa/cm200405/cmselect/cmfaff/113/4101901.htm (follow "Written evidence submitted by Dr. PhilipposSavvides" hyperlink).

Schiff, Amira. 2008. "Prenegotiation and its Limits in Ethno-National Conflicts: A Systematic Analysis of Process and Outcomes in the Cyprus Negotiations." *International Negotiation* 13:388-408.

Simonsen, Sven G. 2009. "Cyprus: Are Old Friends Offering New Hope For Unity?" *CHRISTIAN SCIENCE MONITOR*, May 6. http://www.csmonitor.com/2009/0507/p06s01-woeu.html.

Smith, Helena. 2009. "Scent of Victory Among Lemon Trees as Displaced Cypriots Win Claim on Ancestral Land: Displaced Greek Cypriots Celebrate Landmark Court Ruling on Property Rights,"*GUARDIAN.CO.UK*, May 1. http://www.guardian.co.uk/world/2009/may/01/cyprus-displaced-european-union-greece.

Sozen, Ahmet. 2014. "Solving Cyprus by blending Idealism with Pragmatism," in *Resolving Cyprus: New Approaches to Conflict Resolution* (James Ker-Lindsay, ed., forthcoming, I.B. Tauris).

Spassova, Maria. 2009. "Five Years After Rejecting the Annan Plan, Cyprus is Still Searching for Solutions." *GR REPORTER*, April 23. http://www.grreporter.info/en/node/680.

Stavrinides, Zenon. 2008. "The Underlying Assumptions, Structure and Prospects of the Negotiating Process for a Cyprus Settlement." In *Proceedings of the Sixth International Congress of Cypress [sic] Studies,* ed. Ulker Vanci Osam.

Stavrinides, Zenon. 2009. "Dementia Cypria: On the Social Psychological Environment of the Intercommunal Negotiations." Cyprus Review 21:175-186.

Stavrinides, Zenon. "Cyprus Negotiations: Searching for a Federal Settlement in a Divided Society." (on file with author).

Strauss, Steven D. (2002). *The Complete Idiot's Guide to World Conflicts.* Indianapolis: Penguin/Alpha Books.

Tannen, Deborah. 1987. *That's Not What I Meant: How Conversational Style Makes or Breaks Relationships.* New York: Ballantine.

Tocci, Nathalie. 2006. "Spoiling Peace in Cyprus." In *Challenges to Peacebuilding: Managing Spoilers During Conflict Resolution,"* eds. Edward Newman and Oliver Richmond, 262. New York: United Nations University Press.

Turk, A. Marco. 2006. "Cyprus Reunification is Long Overdue: The Time is Right for Track III Diplomacy as the Best Approach for Successful Negotiation of This Ethnic

Conflict." LOY. L.A. INT'L & COMP. L. REV. 28:205-255.

Turk, A. Marco. 2007. "Rethinking the Cyprus Problem: Are Frame-Breaking Changes Still Possible Through Application of Intractable Conflict Intervention Approaches to This 'Hurting Stalemate'?" LOY. L.A. INT'L & COMP. L. REV. 29:463-501.

Turk, A. Marco. 2008. "Is Cypriot Unification Possible?" *NEW STATESMAN*, August 19. http://www.newstatesman.com/europe/2008/08/cyprus-conflict-cypriots.

Turk, A. Marco. 2009. "The Negotiation Culture of Lengthy Peace Processes: Cyprus as an Example of Spoiling that Prevents a Final Solution." LOY. L.A. INT'L & COMP. L. REV. 31:327-362.

Tzotzadini, Anny. 2010. "Northern Cyprus plans to become Mediterranean 'Las Vegas,'" *GREEK Europe REPORTER*, July 21.http://eu.greekreporter-con/2010/07/21/northern-cyprus-plans-to-become-mediterranean-las-vegas (last visited Oct. 9, 2010).

Umbreit, Mark S. 1997. "Humanistic Mediation: A Transformative Journey of Peacemaking." *Mediation Quarterly* 14: 201-213.

Vance, Cyrus. 1983. *Hard Choices: Critical Years in American Foreign Policy: Memoirs*. New York: Simon and Schuster.

Walker, Anita. 1984. "Enosis in Cyprus: Dhali, a Case Study." *Middle East Journal* 38, 3: 474-494.

Wanis-St. John, Anthony, and Darren Kew. 2008. "Civil Society and Peace Negotiations: Confronting Exclusion." *International Negotiation*13:11.

Winslade, John, and Gerald D. Monk. 2000. *Narrative Mediation: A New Approach to Conflict Resolution.* San Francisco: Jossey-Bass.

Xuequan, Mu. 2009. "Rival Cypriot Communities Accuse Each Other for Lack of Progress on Reunification Talks,"*CHINA VIEW*, January 14. http://news.xinhuanet.com/english/2009-01/14/content_10653309.htm

Xydis, Stephen. 1967. *Cyprus: Conflict and Reconciliation, 1954-1958.* Columbus: Ohio State University Press.

SELECT INDEX

25086913R00122